The Guardian Guide to Working Abroad

Nick Clayton

A & C Black • London

First published in the United Kingdom in 2008 by

A & C Black Publishers Ltd
38 Soho Square
London
W1D 3HB
www.acblack.com

A CIP record for this book is available from the British Library.

ISBN: 9-780-7136-8405-6

This book is produced using paper that is made from wood grown in managed, sustainable forests. It is natural, renewable and recyclable. The logging and manufacturing processes conform to the environmental regulations of the country of origin.

Design by Fiona Pike, Pike Design, Winchester
Typeset by RefineCatch Limited, Bungay, Suffolk
Printed in the United Kingdom by Caligraving

CONTENTS

ACKNOWLEDGEMENTS

In compiling this publication I have trawled through hundreds, if not thousands of websites. The best are, I hope, included at the back of the book. I also read through endless online discussion forums. Without formally taking notes, much of what seemed most useful has been fed into this book almost by a process of osmosis. I'd like to thank all those unsung contributors and ask them to keep on posting. They really do provide the most useful introduction to life in a foreign country and offer unstinting help to new and potential expats.

More specifically, I'd like to thank Monster for guidance on online job hunting; the Fry Group for help with some of the overseas investment information; Claire Laborde for discussing the psychology of settling in; Kevin Harris of Temple Court Chambers for outlining the legal implications of working within the European Union and the Institute for Public Policy Research for its statistics on the numbers of Britons living in particular countries.

Finally I want to thank my wife Barbara, who not only joined me in this risky foreign adventure with its guaranteed lower income and put up with my temper tantrums, but also helped bring together this book, in particular the Web resources at the back.

Nick Clayton - Ibiza
nick@adeskinthesun.com

INTRODUCTION

This book is different from other books about living and working abroad. The others tend to look at one country or the broader mechanics of emigration. This book is for people who feel, for whatever reason, that a move to a different country is what they need. But is it really?

The first part of the book is a quiz which encourages you to look carefully at whether you are really suited to life overseas. Not everybody is, and there's nothing to be ashamed of if you are happy and fulfilled where you are. Indeed, given that the mass movement of people is held responsible for global warming, *not* moving can be seen as a virtue. Equally, if you're unhappy in Britain you can be miserable overseas. The grass isn't always greener or (perhaps more desirably for Brits) more parched by the sun.

Once you've completed the quiz and decided you are ready for the life of an expat, you need to think which country would best suit both your desires and abilities. To begin with you need to establish priorities. It's unlikely, for instance, that you'll find a country which offers you both increased pay and a more relaxed lifestyle. (Let me know if you do.)

Having decided what is most important to you, you can start to ask questions about potential destination countries. To help with your analysis there's a checklist of some of the key points you need to think about. Most are covered in the second section of the book which looks at the individual countries which are most popular with British expats. The aim of the checklist is for you to eliminate all but two or three potential countries in which to make your new home. The final part of the book looks at the issues that people generally face when moving abroad such as taxation, savings and property.

When going through the expat decision-making process, don't forget to involve the other people around you who are going be affected by a move overseas. Somebody who is going to a new job or to set up a business has their life mapped out for them, to a large extent. Partners, children and other relatives don't have that clear focus. They've got to create a new life from scratch, sometimes without obvious personal benefits for them. Even if they're getting to lie by a swimming pool every day in the sunshine, the pleasure may be outweighed by the pain of missing friends from home.

Also, forget looking for the perfect country. Nowhere is free from quirks, foibles and petty bureaucrats whose existence seems designed mainly to make your life difficult. You'll find them all in the land of your birth, but you've probably grown so accustomed to them that you haven't even noticed they are there. A new country will have its own cultural oddities and customs, multiplied because you are now an immigrant and outsider.

Yes, it's not always easy living and working abroad, but it can be incredibly rewarding socially, financially and for your career.

DO YOU REALLY WANT TO MOVE ABROAD?

For many of us in Britain, the actual mechanics of moving abroad are not that difficult, particularly if you stay within the European Union. You sell your house, pay off the mortgage, stick the surplus in the bank and head off. That's really all there is to it, at least to begin with. Most of the problems come later.

The same goes for people who take up the offer of a job overseas or accept a foreign posting from their present employer. There's a great deal you should think about before you make a move, rather than repenting in a strange country when your bridges back to Britain are already burnt.

At the end of the quiz you won't receive a score showing whether you are ideally suited to the life of an expat or not. Sorry, but everybody's personality, skills and motivation is too varied to make that exercise meaningful. The idea is simply to make you think before you leap. Some of the questions will be totally relevant to you, others less so or not at all. As always, do try and involve the other people in your life who'll be affected by the change.

1 How do you generally feel at the end of a two-week holiday?

a Glad to be back in my own bed.

b Sorry it's over, but I made the most of it.

c I didn't ever want it to end.

d I'm looking forward to the next one.

What your answer could mean:

a Obviously you're not going to be that keen on abandoning your present home comforts to move abroad.

b If you want to move abroad, this is probably the right attitude. You would be introducing a large element of uncertainty into your life, which isn't always fun.

c For most expats, life isn't one long holiday, unfortunately. In fact, living abroad can be very hard work with long hours and low pay. Often you're working when everybody else is on holiday.

d Depending on where you move to, life abroad can mean no holidays. When you do get away from your new home, you may find it's just to go and visit friends and relatives in the UK.

2 How concerned are you about job security?

a Who cares? I've got enough in the bank that I'll never have to work again.

b As long as I've got enough to pay for my round it doesn't really matter.

c I want to be sure I can afford this month's rent or mortgage.

d I want to be sure I can afford this year's mortgage.

What your answer could mean:

a Lucky you. There are a few people in this position, but there are risks as well. Countries which were once cheap now match or surpass the UK with their cost of living. Equally, it can get pretty boring doing nothing, even in paradise.

b It must be nice to be so happy-go-lucky. But remember you may be a long way from home without the safety nets of family, friends or social security.

c Striking a happy medium is difficult. In many countries employment is quite seasonal and there'll be times when it's not so easy to find work. Things can always go wrong so make sure you have some sort of rainy-day money in case it all does go pear shaped.

d If you want too much security you'll never leave home. Having a contingency fund that covers your basic living costs for a few months is one thing, guaranteed income is another.

3 How is your health?

a At my last check-up I was told it was very good for my age.
b At my age I can't grumble.
c Spot on. I'm never ill.
d I'm sure a change of climate would do it good.

What your answer could mean:

a Probably the best answer. You're getting your health checked before you set off on a great adventure.
b Are you sure you're up to it?
c Everybody's ill at some point. It's just a matter of time, so get yourself checked over before you move somewhere where you might have to deal with a health service in a foreign language.
d Unless you've got a great deal of money, moving abroad for the sake of your health is a very big risk.

4 How do you feel about your present job?

a I'm good at it and I enjoy the respect it brings.
b It's crap, the same as every other job I've ever had. I can't wait to move on.
c I've got lots of friends at work, but I've probably gone as far as I can.
d Job? What job?

What your answer could mean:

a If you're moving or being posted overseas as a career step, this is probably the right attitude. If you're heading overseas to find work, you

may find that as a foreigner all the respect you used to enjoy will disappear.
b Working in a different country isn't necessarily an improvement, although a crap job in the sun may be better than a crap job in the rain.
c If you feel stale and in need of a change, there are challenges abroad. Beware though, it can be difficult to return and pick up where you left off.
d Maybe you've got nothing to lose, but what are you hoping to find abroad?

5 How is your relationship with your family?

a They all live close by, so there's barely a day goes by when we don't see each other.
b We're not close geographically, but we speak regularly on the phone.
c I'm close to some of them, but there are others I'm never going to speak to again.
d Family? What family?

What your answer could mean:

a Are you sure you could bear to leave them all behind? Abroad can be a very lonely place.
b International phone calls are generally very inexpensive, which should mean it's just as easy for relatives to stay in touch if you're out of the country. But many people find there's a psychological barrier which stops relatives phoning as often when you leave the UK.
c Are you thinking of moving abroad because you want to, or out of spite? It's harder to mend bridges from a long distance.
d If you really feel that, then moving abroad should be no problem.

6 What is your favourite restaurant?

a The cheap, family-run place we go to every week.
b Any McDonalds.

c That romantic spot where we shared lobster and champagne on holiday.
d I'm still looking, but having fun trying to find it.

What your answer could mean:
a This answer suggests you're perhaps not adventurous enough to move abroad. But in plenty of cultures, families have a life-long relationship with a particular restaurant.
b Sadly, you'll probably find one wherever you're planning to move.
c Even if you move to the same area as the restaurant, you probably won't be able to afford to eat there very often and, if you can afford it, you'll find the magic wears off when you're not on holiday.
d Seems like the right answer, but in many countries people are much more patriotic about their cuisine than the Brits so you may not find the amount of choice that you're used to.

7 Some friends invite you to meet up for a social evening. What sort of place would you suggest?
a Somewhere exotic I've never been before.
b A British-run place that will remind us all of home.
c The bar we always go to where everybody knows us.
d I'll let my friends decide.

What your answer could mean:
a Moving to another country can mean a lot less choice than you're used to in the UK, especially if you're escaping the urban rat race and moving to the country.
b If you're that unadventurous, are you sure you want to leave Britain for any length of time?

c It may sound boringly safe, but actually that's what the locals will do in many countries.
d Cop out. Well, why not?

8 What is your ideal Christmas?

a With close family in front of the telly.
b In a quiet spot away from it all with just my partner.
c With all the family – granny, aunts, uncles, nieces, nephews and dozens of cousins.
d Raucous with a load of friends.

What your answer could mean:

a If your close family is already abroad with you, there's no reason why you shouldn't recreate a bit of Britain. Even if you can't get British television channels, there's always the local video shop. Most DVDs have an English language option.
b Provided you're together you could be anywhere.
c This can be difficult. Many people don't realise that the most expensive time to travel is not during the summer holidays, but just before Christmas. It can be a difficult choice between being broke and being lonely.
d This should be easy to arrange. Christmas brings the expats together, although you may find a surprising number somehow manage to get the cash together to return to the UK for the festivities.

9 When did you last give somebody your home phone number?

a It's so long ago, I can't remember.
b I'm never at home, but I give out my mobile number all the time.
c Within the last couple of months.
d I'm always giving out my number.

What your answer could mean:

a Moving abroad means reviving a skill you may not have used since your teens – making friends. And you have to make an effort to keep in touch. Not everybody finds it easy.
b You social butterfly, you! Beware though, it's easy to get a 'reputation' – i.e. be thought of as too easy – in the close-knit expat community.
c Well, you probably haven't lost the knack of making new friends.
d Good. But you still have to make the effort to phone people as well.

10 What's your favourite way of spending an evening?

a In front of the telly with a pizza.
b Over a relaxing meal with friends.
c At the cinema or theatre.
d Out clubbing until dawn.

What your answer could mean:

a You think you're going to be accused of being unadventurous and, therefore, not suited to a life abroad. In fact, telly and pizza are just about universal so you can enjoy them anywhere.
b Being sociable is a vital part of making the most of being abroad. And what better way than a meal with friends?
c In many countries you'll struggle to find entertainment in English. DVDs usually have a choice of language, but it's not the same as going to the cinema. It's very easy to become detached from your culture.
d You may be able to do that on holiday, but it's not always easy if you've got work the following day.

11 How do you react when bureaucrats make your life difficult?

a I give them a good earful. It might not help, but it makes me feel better.
b I keep at them until the problem's resolved.

c I ask around and look online in case there's another way round the problem.

d Ignore them. Life's too short.

What your answer could mean:

a And you can do that in a foreign language?

b Probably a laudable attitude, but in some countries you might be more constructively employed banging your head against a real brick wall.

c This is probably the best way. Just make sure the advice you get is reliable.

d Unfortunately, this is what many Brits do and it can leave you with trouble piled up in the end.

12 Where do most of your friends come from?

a I went to school with most of them.

b Now I think about it, most of them are from work.

c I've got friends from all over the place – work, the pub, the gym, I can't remember.

d I don't really go in for lots of friends; my partner gives me everything I need in the way of companionship.

What your answer could mean:

a Move abroad and you'll have to make new friends. Can you do it?

b You'll be leaving them behind. And you may find working relationships abroad are very different.

c You should make friends if you move abroad as well, but there aren't always the same social hubs available as there are in the UK.

d Great, if it's true. Moving abroad can put a great deal of strain on a relationship and having nobody else to talk to can add to the pressure.

13 If you moved abroad, what sort of friends would you hope to make?

- a Mostly locals. I hate the thought of the whole expat scene.
- b People from the UK. They're the only ones who really understand where I come from.
- c Whoever drinks in the local bar.
- d It's not something I've really thought about. I'd just play it by ear.

What your answer could mean:

- a Even if you're fluent in the language, it's not always as straightforward as it sounds. Particularly in rural areas, you may find that the extended family is the centre of social life. You don't have one with you.
- b You may be missing out on local culture, but Brits have run their own social scene since even before the days of the Raj.
- c You may want to avoid becoming that sad cultural stereotype, the alcoholic expat.
- d This is probably the best attitude. You don't really know how your social life is going to develop until you've moved.

14 Have you ever been to a social event in Britain with somebody who'd be classed as from an 'ethnic minority'?

- a I don't think I know any.
- b There are a few people at work, but they prefer to keep to their own kind, don't they?
- c I love going to events where I'm the one in the ethnic minority.
- d I've been to one or two events, but I felt a bit uncomfortable.

What your answer could mean:

- a In most countries you'll be part of an ethnic minority.
- b Would you be happy moving to a place where the locals treat you that way?

c If you're telling the truth, you should enjoy moving to another country.
d If you live abroad, you may have to get used to feeling uncomfortable.

15 What would you normally find in your shopping basket?

a Mostly prepared British food, nothing too exotic.
b Mostly ready meals, the more exotic the better.
c Generally vegetarian, a mixture of ready meals and other stuff.
d Nothing processed if I can avoid it. I love to cook.

What your answer could mean:

a Sounds as if you're a bit unadventurous, and prepared food's not generally as popular as it is in the UK.
b Few countries have the selection of exotic ready meals that you'll find in British supermarkets. If you're not up to cooking for yourself, you may find local food a bit boring.
c If you're used to slinging a prepared veggie meal in the microwave you'll be disappointed in most countries outside the UK.
d Wherever you are, you'll find something to cook and enjoy.

16 When on holiday abroad, do you hire a car and go off exploring?

a No. I'm a bit nervous about driving in another country.
b No. I always stay in cities where I don't need a car.
c Yes, of course. It's the only way to escape from the other tourists.
d I can't drive.

What your answer could mean:

a It may be understandable, but unless you live in a city you're likely to feel rather isolated unless you drive. Are you sure you're ready to move?
b Fair enough. But some cities are a struggle without a car.

c It's the same when you move abroad permanently.
d Maybe you're being environmentally conscientious, but maybe you're relying on friends and relatives too much. They won't be there if you move.

17 What do you think of credit cards?

a They're more convenient than cash and I usually pay them off within a couple of months.
b They're too convenient. I earn just about enough each month to cover the minimum payment on all my cards.
c I never use them. I hate to be in debt of any sort.
d I've cut all mine up and I should have all the debt paid off in about six months.

What your answer could mean:

a If you've got the self-control, this is probably the healthiest attitude to debt. However, Britain makes more use of credit cards than just about any country, so you may not be able to manage your finances in quite the same way if you move abroad.
b It's not impossible to carry on in the same way if you move abroad, but it's often very difficult. Getting credit from a foreign bank can be much harder than in the UK especially for the first few years until you've established yourself as a 'good risk'.
c Congratulations. You can obviously carry on along the same route if you move. The only difficulty might be if you run into some teething problems; a little short-term borrowing could then be the best way to see you through.
d Good move. It's still a good idea to wait until your good intentions have turned into a positive bank balance. You don't want to end up in the same position, but with the added difficulty of being in a foreign country.

18 How do you and your partner get on?

a I don't have a partner.

b Great. We always agree.

c Of course we have our differences and sometimes we argue, but we always sort things out in the end.

d A change of pace and place would help us sort our relationship out.

What your answer could mean:

a Being on your own means you have nobody to disagree with, which can make life easier. On the other hand, a foreign country can be a very lonely place.

b At first that sounds perfect. But moving is a hard decision and you really need to be sure that both of you really want to do it. If one of you is just going along with the idea to avoid arguments then you could well be storing up problems for the future when the going gets tough.

c Even healthy relationships can buckle under the strain of moving to a different country. But if you can keep talking through your problems you should be okay.

d Moving overseas to strengthen a rocky relationship is probably the second-worst thing you can do. (The worst is having a baby.)

19 How long have you and your partner been together?

a I don't have a partner.

b Less than a year.

c More than a year, but less than a decade.

d For ever!

What your answer could mean:

a Assuming you're not running away from a previous relationship, travelling alone has much to recommend it. But it can be lonely.

b Make sure you have an escape route. Nothing tests a relationship like a move to a new country.
c You should know each other well enough by now to cope with the change. The only thing to consider is motive. Are you trying to spice up a relationship which was ready to die?
d It's always good to hear of a relationship that lasts. Love is definitely the answer. The question is whether you've really grown together or if the thought of a move is just a way to relieve the boredom.

20 As you come to the end of this quiz, are you thinking . . .?

a I'm not so sure if I really want to move abroad.
b Nothing's going to keep me in this miserable, damp and boring country.
c The quiz has given me a few things to think about, but I'm pretty sure I'd like to move abroad.
d Why think? I believe in spontaneity so I'll just grab a flight when I feel like it.

What your answer could mean:

a Emigrating is not easy and it's not for everybody. That's just as well, because somebody has to stay behind. Seriously, if you're really not sure, don't do it.
b If you're fed up and bored in Britain, there's a fair chance you'll feel the same way in another country. Heading abroad is certainly not a solution to all your problems and nowhere's been perfect since God chucked Adam and Eve out of Paradise.
c Well, keep looking. Why not try posting a message on one of the many online discussion forums listed at the back of this book or found through a search engine such as Google. There's no better way of finding out if and where you want to move than by making contact with

other people who are thinking of the same thing or who have already set up home abroad.

d There are people who've successfully emigrated just on a whim. Equally, there are those who've regretted that they didn't spend a little more time thinking about what they were going to do. Think about what you might be giving up.

Once you've finished this little quiz, and assuming you haven't been totally put off the idea of moving, it's time to think about where to move to. The world may be your oyster, but that doesn't mean you've found the pearl.

WHERE TO NEXT?

Having decided that you are suited to a move abroad, the next obvious question is – where? But before you try and work that one out, you really need to know *why*. What's your motivation for creating this huge upheaval in your life and the lives of the people around you?

What this section attempts to do is provide a logical framework for deciding which country would best suit you. It may be at the end of the process you decide to ignore logic and go with a gut instinct. To be honest, that's probably what I'd do. Choosing where to live generally has as much to do with logic as does selecting a marriage partner. But in either case, if you can justify your choice, so much the better.

Everybody has different reasons for moving abroad. It's worthwhile deciding what your priorities are so at least you can rule out some places.

ELEVEN PLUS ONE KEY REASONS FOR MOVING ABROAD

1. **Career progression.** There may be more prospects abroad in your profession, or a period spent overseas might benefit your CV.

2. **Higher pay.** Your skills may be more highly regarded and rewarded in another country.

3. **Sunnier climate.** Who wants to wait for global warming?

4. **Lower prices.** Your income will go further.

5. **Cheaper housing.** Few countries have seen house prices rocket the way they have in the UK. You may be able to sell up, buy the home of your dreams and have enough left over to start a business.

6. **A better environment for children.** Whether it's the thought of lower crime levels, natural bilingualism or a healthier lifestyle, many people move for the sake of their kids.

7. **Relaxed lifestyle.** Escaping the rat race is a common motive for a move abroad.

8. **Setting up your own business.** It's not usually an easy option, but the dream of being your own boss in a place in the sun is increasingly popular.

9. **Less taxation.** Although the British Chancellor actually takes a lower slice of income than in many countries, there are still places where you can take home more of your pay.

10. **Scenery.** How important is it to you to wake up to beauty every morning, or are some of the other elements rather more important?

11. **Skills.** Does the country you want to go to need the knowledge, experience and qualifications you possess? Can you make a living?

+1 **Love.** Not every Shirley Valentine or her male equivalent decides to stay in the UK. But if romance is your motive, you've presumably chosen your destination already.

CHOOSING YOUR COUNTRY

Why are you here? I mean, why are you living and working where you do now? Was it a conscious decision or did it just happen? The fact that you're reading this book suggests that you are in some way dissatisfied with your current situation.

There are people who claim to have a clearly mapped-out career plan, but they are few and far between. And many of them probably developed their maps with hindsight, having reached an exalted position. The rest of us end up in our particular jobs and homes thanks to a mixture of inertia, relationships, luck, coincidence and possibly a little bit of skill.

Before you disrupt your life – and the lives of the people around you – it is obviously best to try and avoid repeating mistakes. Moving country can offer the opportunity to make a carefully considered decision. That's the aim of this section, to help you decide which country best suits your needs and abilities.

The idea here is to compare two or more possible destinations. Go through the questions below and create a list of the positives and negatives of each country you're considering. A checklist or simple spreadsheet will let you see your answers at a glance

WHAT IS THE CLIMATE LIKE ALL THE YEAR ROUND?

Everybody gets fed up with the British weather at some point. But make sure you really know what the climate is going to be like in your intended destination. You may have been visiting it every summer since you were a child, but those glorious summers may be offset by long, damp winters. Alternatively, guaranteed dry sunshine might leave you desperate for the coolness of a green meadow.

Sadly, there's no such thing as a perfect climate. Just try and make sure you really know what you want. And make sure the part of the country you're planning to move to measures up. Microclimates can cause huge variations even within a fairly small region. Andalucia in southern Spain, for instance, contains the country's wettest, driest and hottest places.

JUST HOW EXOTIC IS THE WILDLIFE?

Beyond wasp stings and nettle rash there's not too much in the way of nasties in the UK, well, not unless global warming has a huge impact. Some other countries have an abundance of things that sting, bite and give you infectious diseases. If you're the sort of person who lives in perpetual fear of a spider in the bath, there are some countries that might not suit you.

HOW EASY IS IT TO GET TO AND GET BACK?

Maybe we're living in the golden age of cheap air travel. At the moment many places are cheap to get to, even if the flight itself is fairly long. With concerns about the impact of air travel on global warming, however, it seems likely there will be more surcharges on fuel that's already rising in price and the combination will substantially increase the price of tickets over the coming years. This is worth bearing in mind if you are considering relocation to a place that's a long-haul flight away and you have to come back to Britain on a regular basis.

Before then, look to see just how reliable connections are. Budget airlines have rushed to tie up routes to what are relatively out-of-the-way airports, but where landing fees are low. The operators can quickly reduce frequency or even drop destinations altogether when they cease to be profitable. If work or family commitments require frequent visits to the UK or elsewhere, it would be a real problem if suddenly the nearest airport was several hours' drive away. It's even worse if you've moved to an island.

Although nothing can ever be certain, it is worth ensuring that the nearest airport to your new home is served by several airlines, both budget and full service. It's less likely they'll all drop a route. Alternatively, look to move somewhere with more than one airport within reasonable distance.

HOW MUCH DOES PROPERTY COST AND HOW GOOD IS IT?

One of the most common mistakes made by new expats is to be seduced by a bargain property. Yes, you might be able to trade in your suburban semi for a self-contained castle with a swimming pool, but have you looked at the practicalities?

Houses in the UK are, generally, designed to be easy to maintain. Life isn't usually a constant battle with nature, leaking roofs, dry rot, wet rot, dodgy plumbing, algae in the swimming pool, erratic electricity supplies and a phone service that you're continually promised will be connected one day.

More importantly, you should make sure you know what the price of property is in the place where you are going to be able to earn your living. A house isn't a bargain if you can't afford its upkeep.

WHAT WOULD YOUR COST OF LIVING BE LIKE?

It is very difficult to make a meaningful comparison between countries as far as prices are concerned. Individual lifestyle makes such a difference. You really need to think about how you are planning to live and work.

If, for instance, you are planning to work as a 'digital nomad', providing services for organisations remote from where you are going to live, you really need to know the cost and reliability of Internet and other telecommunications services. The cost of travel may be more or less than it was in the UK, depending on whether you've been able to escape from commuting. You may be able to do without many of the comforts of home in Britain, from Cadbury's chocolate to Heinz beans, but maybe not.

Prices anyway are relative: what seems cheap on an income of £50,000 a year looks expensive if you're only bringing in a fifth of that. Try to make a realistic appraisal of your relative cost of living set against your lowest expected income.

It stands to reason that the real cost of living in a country comes from measuring prices against income. Property, food and essentials may be cheap by UK standards, but how do they compare with the income you expect to receive?

HOW MUCH IS IT GOING TO COST YOU TO MOVE?

It's amazing how few people work out how much the act of moving is going to cost, assuming you're not getting it as part of a relocation package. Some of us know through bitter experience that, for instance, living on an island can lead to surcharges on removal costs that are several times more than they would be to a mainland destination.

HOW EASY WILL IT BE TO FIND WORK?

It may seem obvious, but make sure you know what the employment prospects are in your destination of choice. Many popular destinations have high levels of unemployment and, unless you have highly specialised skills and qualifications, you're going to find locals at the front of the queue.

If you do have qualifications from the UK, make sure they are accepted in your new country without the need for additional verification. Australia, for example, is short of skilled trades people, but fulfilling the requirement for practical proof of ability can mean facing several months without an income.

COULD YOU START YOUR OWN BUSINESS THERE?

Many people dream of setting up a business in a new country. Unfortunately, many don't wake up from their dreams before moving. Most new businesses fail. That's a fact in any country and it applies to the people who have been brought up with the local practices and bureaucracy. What chance have you got as a foreigner?

Actually, prospects of success might be better than they seem at first glance. The level of immigration is a good indicator of the dynamism of a local economy. There are many success stories from foreigners who have spotted gaps in the market and exploited them. But there are far more people who have not looked carefully at their business plan to see whether it has a realistic chance of working.

There are probably reasons why particular goods and services are not available in a place. Not enough people want them. Equally, popularity can be sign of saturation rather than overwhelming demand. Anybody launching a business in Britain would carry out market research. It's more difficult abroad, but it's certainly no less important.

IS THERE SUPPORT FOR NEW BUSINESSES?

Some countries positively encourage start-ups, while others put no end of bureaucratic obstacles in their way. Swimming against this tide may seem brave, but it's more likely to be foolhardy. Use Google or another search engine to find expat business discussion forums or look at the list at the back of this book. The best people to ask about setting up and running a business are those that have already done it.

HOW MUCH TAX WILL YOU HAVE TO PAY?

There's still an assumption that Britain has a high tax economy. It hasn't. In most other countries the state will take a bigger slice of your pay packet. Straightforward comparisons between tax regimes are seldom possible. You can see what the headline rate is, but that doesn't take into account allowances, thresholds and just how tough the authorities are. You should take advice from a local tax expert, but also talk to other people who are already doing your sort of work in your potential new home country.

DO YOU HAVE THE RIGHT LANGUAGE SKILLS?

We should all learn the language of the country we choose to make our home, but don't assume it'll be quick or easy. It is an awful lot simpler if large numbers of people speak English. Deciding how important this is to you is a matter of being honest with yourself. Many expats end up feeling very isolated because they can do no more than mumble and smile at their friendly neighbours.

HOW CLOSE IS THE GOVERNMENT TO YOUR BELIEFS?

Many expats pay little attention to the people running the country they live in. They probably didn't play an active part in British politics either. There are, however, some pretty nasty regimes running places with substantial British expat populations living in them. You may think you'll be comfortable with the oppression, but it's better to think about it in advance than when it affects you directly.

HOW STABLE IS THE COUNTRY POLITICALLY?

Coming from the UK it's easy to take political stability very much for granted. But it's unusual. Most countries have lived through violent upheaval of some degree within living memory. As with oppressive governments, it's worth doing a little research before you move. Getting caught up in a revolution might provide you with some good stories for your grandchildren, but leaving somewhere with just the clothes you stand up in isn't so good for the bank balance.

WHAT IS THE STANDARD AND COST OF HEALTHCARE?

Unusually, this is an area where Brits tend to think their country scores more highly than it does, and in fact many countries have overtaken Britain with the quality of care for their population. You should look at both the quality and price of healthcare in the country you are considering making your home, especially if you expect your stay to extend into retirement.

WHAT IS THE STANDARD AND COST OF EDUCATION?

People moving abroad with children have three basic educational choices. They can go with the local school system. They can send their kids to the local international school, if there is one. Or they can pack off their children back to a UK boarding school. See p.173 for the pros and cons of the different options. But, for people with children, the quality, price and availability of schools is a key element in deciding where to move.

HOW IMPORTANT IS CULTURE?

To some extent it's as much to do with urban versus rural or city versus provincial, but if certain types of what's called 'culture' are an important part of your life, you could find a move leaving a big hole in your existence. Cinema and theatre are not the same in a foreign language and DVD is not film. Looking at local papers and online expat forums should give you some guide as to whether your sort of culture is important in your potential destination.

FRANCE

Logically, France should be the major destination for emigrating Brits. For most of the UK's population, it's closer than Scotland. The French speak a language which the majority of us have some limited experience of at school, and we've been nipping back and forth across each other's borders since humanity discovered how to build and paddle a boat.

These days there are assorted British tribes in France. There are the Peter Mayle followers in Provence, the cross-channel commuters in the north and others dotted about around the country. But somehow France doesn't have the mass Brit-appeal of Spain or Australia. This may be down to the certain cultural antipathy between England and France. This isn't really shared by the Scots and Welsh, who perhaps harbour some of the same feelings as the French towards the English. More important, perhaps, is the size of the country which makes much of it relatively inaccessible from the UK. If it were as easy to jump on a cheap flight to the south of France as it is to the Spanish *costas*, perhaps it would be more popular.

The lack of a big expat community may, however, be an attraction for people who want to get away from Brits as well as Britain: there are large swathes of the country where you'll never hear English spoken.

QUICK FACTS

- **Land area:** At 549,000 square kilometres, France is the largest country in Western Europe.
- **Population:** 62,752,136
- **Climate:** In the north and northwest – Normandy, Ile de France, Picardy and Brittany – the climate is similar to the south of England. Eastern and central France have warmer summers and colder winters. The south and southwest have a Mediterranean climate with occasionally cold winters and often very hot summers.

- **Main language:** French
- **Currency:** The euro (£1 = €1.33, January 2008)
- **How long does it take to get there from the UK and are services year round?** As Britain's closest continental neighbour, geographically at least, there are a wide variety of options – trains, planes and the Channel Tunnel for anybody wanting to reach the north of the country quickly. Cross-border commuting is possible, although it would be more than a little stressful on body and wallet. It is, however, a realistic option for people who have regular meetings in London but don't want to pay Home Counties property prices, or who prefer the Gallic lifestyle.

  Getting to the centre and south of the country can prove a little more problematic for anybody who needs to visit the UK regularly, quickly and fairly cheaply. There are scheduled flights to the main centres of population, but they can prove expensive. Budget airlines do serve these areas as well. It would be foolish to base a move on the availability of cheap flights though as the no-frills carriers have a tendency to change frequency on routes or even drop them altogether. This can happen at very short notice.
- **How many British migrants are there and where do they live mostly?** There are about 200,000 Britons living in France with clusters in Paris, close to the French Channel in the north and in the southwest.
- **Cost of living.** It's quite common to hear that France is around 25 per cent cheaper than the UK. As ever, that depends on how the comparison is made. Economists take a 'common basket of goods' as their standard measure, so it all depends whether you buy the same collection of products and services. Most expats seem to agree that the cost of smoking, drinking and running a car – not simultaneously – is probably cheaper than Britain. Other differences are less marked. On the other hand, unemployment is higher and pay is lower, so the net effect for many expats is that their real cost of living is higher.

THE ECONOMY

In many ways the French economy would appear to be a model of success. Growth ahead of the European average through the 1990s was accompanied by the introduction of the 35-hour week in a country with the lowest poverty and income inequality rates of any of the world's major economies.

Against that, unemployment has remained resolutely above seven per cent and growth has been fairly weak since the turn of the millennium. But France is still the world's sixth largest economy and the third largest in Europe behind Germany and the UK.

A series of right-wing governments have failed to significantly liberalise France's labour laws or reduce the relatively high minimum wage. Despite evidence to the contrary, the public perception is of substantial pockets of poverty. This is partly fuelled by the contrast between people in safe, well-paid jobs and those in seemingly intractable positions of unemployment. The Sarkozy government was elected in 2007 with a mandate to further liberalise the economy.

Part of the problem may be the traditional nature of the French economy. While other countries have seen their heavy industries decline, France is still deeply reliant on agriculture. In fact it's the largest agricultural producer in the EU, responsible for a third of total output. Globally, only the USA is a larger producer.

The importance of food and drink to France isn't that unexpected. What's a little more surprising is the size of the country's tourism industry. According to the World Tourism Organization, France received over 75 million tourists in 2004, which is over 20 million more than Spain, the second-highest ranked country. A hopefully unrelated statistic is that France is the third largest arms supplier in the world.

Income tax in France is relatively low, especially for the low-paid in larger families. That's because it's assessed on a household rather than an individual basis, which makes it hard to make comparisons with Britain. Other taxes and national insurance contributions can be a little quirky, as we'll see later.

DOING BUSINESS IN FRANCE

The French are perhaps a little more formal in their business dealings than the British. They also tend to separate their business and social lives to a greater extent. Attitudes, however, are changing and while it's certainly best to dress and act conservatively at an initial meeting you may be able to be more casual subsequently.

Language is very important. At least try to use some French even if the people you are dealing with speak good English. Use the formal *vous* until the relationship has matured. The same goes for first names.

Although in some ways the French can seem almost too polite, they can be very blunt when asking questions. Perhaps because philosophy forms part of their national school curriculum they're often impressed by debating skills. It is, however, a risky strategy to employ your full rhetorical armoury at a meeting. The line between a debate and an argument is a fine one.

Any agreement is likely to be written out in an extremely detailed form and may not follow directly from a meeting. The French speak face-to-face to discuss issues, not to reach decisions.

WORK AND JOBS

It remains to be seen what long-term impact the liberalising agenda of the Sarkozy government will have on jobs. Currently legislation ensures that workers enjoy relatively high levels of job security, which makes it expensive for companies to fire people or make them redundant. Arguably, this has made employers reluctant to recruit staff and has led to a fairly high level of unemployment in recent years.

There *are* jobs for British expats with the right skills, but they are not always easy to come by. They are also often considerably less well paid than they are in the UK. It goes almost without saying that almost all professional jobs require a high degree of fluency in French.

If you want to be sure of a job before you leave the UK, there are a couple of options. Some posts are advertised in the UK quality press and you can also register with a recruitment agency. Or you can, of course, access French websites (see p. 196) whether for agencies or specific companies advertising vacancies. The chances are, however, that if you meet their requirements you'll be expected to be available for interview. That's easier once you've made the move.

Once there, you'll find cities in France have the equivalent of Job Centres, known often by their acronym 'ALE' (Agence Local pour Emploi). These are part of the *Agence National pour l'Emploi* (ANPE). As with their UK counterparts, these tend to be geared to less skilled employment, but some cities have specialised agencies for managerial staff called 'Espaces Cadres'. Once in France you can register as a jobseeker at one of the ANPE offices and consult advertisements online at www.anpe.fr. You can also sign up to receive details of vacancies matching your profile.

Temp agencies play perhaps a more important role in the French job market than they do in the UK because of the tough employment protection laws which make companies reluctant to recruit staff unless it's absolutely necessary. The agencies are well regulated so it's worth registering, as long, of course, as you have good language skills. It might not lead straight to a permanent job, but it will provide local proof of your abilities.

The same goes for language teaching where there is a growing demand for people, the more qualified the better. It's not uncommon to start working part time for a number of schools with, perhaps, a bit of private tuition thrown in. Eventually you could end up on the staff of one of them.

In France, perhaps more than most countries, many jobs are simply not advertised. It's not pure nepotism because you don't always have to be related to the boss, but it does help if you know them socially. So take advantage of every networking opportunity (see pp. 168–72) and don't be afraid to ask the people you meet if they know of any jobs available.

STARTING A BUSINESS

The alternative to finding a job is to be self employed. That is not always an easy option, however, and many Brits complain that although 'entrepreneur' is a French word, it is not a French concept. Bureaucracy and taxation can be a nightmare, with fixed deductions often based on projections of future earnings.

It's all a contrast to the relatively liberal regime enjoyed by people who work for themselves in Britain. Income tax and national insurance are at least roughly in line with how much is earned. Provided it's legal, the authorities aren't really bothered where the money comes from. In fact, perhaps the most common route into UK self-employment is through 'bootstrapping', where people continue to earn using an established skill while they build up their new business.

In France, somebody trying that could find themselves paying two *cotisations* – the rough equivalent of national insurance. It's part of a system that seems very rigid to many expats. If you have a specific skill you have to be accepted by and join the appropriate professional organisation in order to pay tax and contributions. And don't even think of working 'on the black'. The government has really clamped down on the black economy and both users and providers of untaxed services risk fines and even prison.

IT CAN BE DONE

It's not impossible to run a business from France, as Andy Turner found out. As with so many people (including me), his move reflected a need for change. He's Yorkshire-born, as is his wife Jenny, but had lived in a leafy part of London for 15 years. The last eight years had been spent running his own successful public relations consultancy.

Andy and Jenny had bought a property in Cessenon-sur-Orb, Languedoc, in the south of France as a holiday home. 'I'd been working here for six to eight weeks over the summer,' he told me from his French home. 'We thought: "Why not move here lock stock from London?" '

In fact, they've hung on to their London property, which they now rent out. 'I'd advise anybody, if they can, to have at least two income streams that are not interdependent,' he said. It goes some way to reducing the risk.

Moving his business turned out to be more complex than Andy had thought. What seemed the simplest solution – retaining his UK company – just wasn't possible. Also the advice he received from his UK accountants proved not to be totally accurate. It's a common problem for emigrants, finding financial advisors who understand business procedures under two legislations as well as the peculiarities of specific trades and professions. An added complexity of the French tax system is that it's based on household, rather than individual, income.

Fortunately, through word of mouth, Andy was able to find two English-speaking accountants. In the end he opted for one in Le Havre, despite the distance, because the practice had more experience in this area. With the advice of the accountant, he decided to register as a self-employed professional. The alternative would have been to set up a small company known as an SARL or EURL.

Either way, Andy warns people setting up in France to be sure to have all their papers together well in advance. The authorities even needed to see his parents' birth certificates, even though they're in their eighties. They'll also ask very detailed questions about where work will be carried out, expected income and plans for growth. That's why it was so important to have an accountant who was able to explain the nuances of the questions in English as it requires a very high standard of French to understand the official requirements.

Completing all the paperwork and having it accepted is really only the beginning. After three years there's a reckoning by the authorities and a correction in the amount of tax owed. Many expat businesses collapse under the pressure of the resulting bill.

Although Andy and Jenny Turner have had some long soul-searching discussions, they feel that the move to France has been worthwhile. When the time comes for their young daughter to go to school in France, it will be less of a gamble than the English system. The same is true of the French health service. And there's those 300 days of sunshine a year.

Andy does have advice for people planning a similar move. He says they should develop a relationship with a French bank as soon as possible: setting up an account can be slow. He also recommends making sure that IT is in place before the move, otherwise it means relying, as he did, on the goodwill of clients.

The transitional period is bound to be difficult as it's a time when you have to keep an existing business going while dealing with intense bureaucracy. Often the greatest help will come from friends you've made who've done the same thing as you. That doesn't mean it's not important to make local friends.

He also says it's vital to have a 'crunch fund' for the inevitable crises. The Turner's car engine blew up just at the end of its warranty period at almost the same time as they found their house was being eaten by termites.

'You should go in with your eyes open,' he said. What he's not certain about is careful planning. Although by nature prudent, he admits there are some people who plunge in and survive. Others are doomed to disappointment when things don't go as expected.

ACCOMMODATION AND PROPERTY

Compared with the ridiculously high property prices in the UK, those in France can seem unbelievably cheap. That is good news for people planning a long-term move to the country. Others should be wary. Traditionally, property in France has not been seen as an investment. The size of the country means there has been room to expand so there haven't been shortages to drive up prices. At the same time the private rented sector is large, representing around a quarter of households.

This may change following the victory of the conservative Sarkozy government in 2007, with its commitment to creating a property-owning democracy. It seems unlikely, however, that any impact will be that rapid, as it will have to overcome attitudes that have been entrenched for many years. Assuming the slow rise in house prices continues, it will probably take several years before the profit on the sale of a property will cover the legal and other costs associated with the initial purchase. That may be particularly true of what seem to be real bargains. The romantic, isolated farmhouse was probably cheap to buy because the locals weren't interested and there's no reason for them to change their minds simply because you need to move.

The alternative to selling a property is to let it out. With such a large and vibrant rental sector, this may seem to be an attractive option, especially if otherwise you'd be losing money on the sale. You should also take professional advice from an accountant before you go down this route as it has implications for capital gains tax, both in the UK and France, if you own or sell properties in either or both countries.

WORKING IN THE EUROPEAN UNION

Every citizen of the European Union has the right to work and live in another member state without being discriminated against on grounds of nationality. This includes the right to:

- look for a job
- work
- reside in that member state for work
- remain there

It also includes the right to equal treatment in respect of access to employment, working conditions and all other advantages which could help to facilitate the worker's integration in the host member state. Free movement of self-employed workers is also guaranteed through treaty provisions on freedom of establishment and freedom to provide services.

Family members have the right to live with the worker in the host member state and the right to equal treatment as regards, for example, education and social advantages. Some family members also have the right to work there.

As a national of an EU country, you may look for a job in any other EU member state and be given assistance by the national employment offices. According to the European Court of Justice, a jobseeker may stay in the host state for a period 'sufficient to enable him to appraise himself of offers of employment and to take the necessary steps to be engaged'. At the end of this period, you cannot be kicked out if you can show you're continuing to seek employment and you have a genuine chance of getting a job.

You no longer need to obtain a residence permit if you're working in an EU country, but if you're going to be working for less than three months, you may be asked to notify the authorities of your presence. When employment is expected to last *more* than three months, you may have to register with the relevant authority. In this case, a registration certificate should be issued immediately upon production of a passport and a job confirmation from your employer or a certificate of employment. You can't be asked for other documents such as payslips, electricity bills or tax statements. You do not have to wait until you're registered to start work.

As a worker who has lived continuously for five years in an EU member state, you automatically have the right of permanent residence in that country. Upon request, the national authorities should issue a document certifying permanent residence. Once acquired, the right of permanent residence may be lost only if you leave the country for a period of more than two consecutive years.

Any EU citizen has the right to take up an activity in another member state under the same conditions as apply to its own nationals. Quotas are illegal. The only discrimination that's allowed is that employers are allowed to stipulate a certain level of linguistic ability, provided that it is reasonable and necessary for the job in question.

The recruitment of Community nationals may not be restricted in number or percentage, nor depend on criteria which are discriminatory by comparison with those applied to nationals. An exception applies for linguistic knowledge: a certain level of language may be required for a job.

When working in another member state, your conditions – for example, pay, dismissal and reinstatement – must be exactly the same as local colleagues. You're entitled to equal access to training. You also have the right to the same social and tax advantages as national workers, for instance, public transport fare reductions for large families, child raising allowances, minimum subsistence payments and so on.

Article 39(4) of the EC treaty says that the free movement of workers does not apply to employment in the public sector. This means that access to the public service may be restricted to nationals of the host member state, but the article isn't quite as restrictive as it sounds. Only those posts in which the exercise of public authority and the responsibility for safeguarding the general interest of the state is involved may be restricted to their own nationals. These criteria must be evaluated in a case-by-case approach in view of the nature of the tasks and responsibilities covered by the post in question.

Recruitment must therefore be open to all EU citizens unless the posts meet these strict criteria. And if you do get a job, you can't be treated differently from the locals.

Previous periods of comparable professional experience in another EU country must be taken into account as far a getting a public service job is concerned and for determining pay levels or grades.

A less well publicised piece of legislation, 'Decision No 2241/2004/EC', to give its official title, established a European standard curriculum vitae. Don't laugh. It stipulates everything, right down to the layout and font.

Actually, its aims are quite laudable and the website for the 'Europass' (www.uknec.org.uk) is actually quite useful. It provides an online form which you are guided through step by step until you've created your perfectly-formatted CV, which can be downloaded to print or e-mail according to what's required for your job application. The document would actually be just as useful for any post you happened to be applying for, even if it was in Asia rather than Europe. It's also easy to adapt so you can fit the CV to match the vacancy.

The CV is just one part of the Europass. It also includes: a language passport to describe your linguistic skills; a mobility record to record any period spent learning or training in a European country; a certificate supplement to explain the meaning of vocational training from one country to another; a diploma supplement to help people outside the issuing country to understand degree and diploma qualifications.

GERMANY

There was a time in the 1970s and 1980s when capitalist West Germany had an almost magnetic attraction. It was embedded deeply enough in the British psyche to become the basis of one of the most successful television drama series of the period, *Auf Wiedersehen, Pet*. At that time – in stark contrast to Britain – jobs in Germany were plentiful and well paid.

Those differences have gone now. The financial attractions have disappeared with reunification and a sluggish economy. But there are still tens of thousands of British people in Germany who are actually perhaps better integrated than elsewhere. Certainly the conspicuous signs of cafes serving British beer, Sunday roasts and all-day breakfast fry-ups are nowhere to be seen.

QUICK FACTS

- **Land area:** 357,021 square kilometres
- **Population:** 83 million
- **Climate:** Although the country is broadly temperate, there are variations. The east, for instance, is generally colder in winter. Round the Rhine, meanwhile, the summers are warm enough to cultivate vines.
- **Main language:** German
- **Currency:** The euro (£1 = €1.33, January 2008)
- **How long does it take to get there from the UK and are services year round?** Flight times are around one-and-a-half to two hours depending on departure and arrival airports. As Germany isn't a major holiday destination, there is little difference in frequency of flights at different times of the year. Driving from Calais would probably take a little more than three hours to get to the German border and another five hours or so to travel east to Berlin.
- **How many British migrants are there and where do they live mostly?** There are around 115,000 British passport holders living in Germany.

- **Cost of living:** The former West Germany used to be regarded as very expensive compared with the UK. Now it is generally comparable in price for most goods and services. The old East Germany remains relatively cheap; in fact, one survey showed Leipzig to be the cheapest city in Europe.

THE ECONOMY

The German economy is the largest in Europe, however it has been notoriously sluggish for a number of years. Partly that's because its greatest strength is also its greatest weakness: exports account for over a third of national output, but that makes the economy vulnerable to external difficulties.

There have been continuing problems stemming from the reunification with the former East Germany. Some people also blame some of the country's economic woes on the highly regulated labour market. Those people also blame the quantity of red tape for the difficulties there are in starting new businesses. Consumer confidence has also been wobbly, creating a reluctance to get into individual debt which has restricted domestic demand.

For such a developed economy Germany has a surprisingly large industrial sector, representing over a quarter of employment and GDP. It's the third largest producer of motor vehicles after the USA and Japan (although China's coming close), and also produces nearly 20 per cent of the world's machine tools - more than any other country.

Tourism may not be immediately synonymous with Germany, but it represents eight per cent of its GDP. Business travellers make up a large proportion of that figure: two-thirds of all major trade fairs are held in the country, attracting up to 10 million visitors.

The most generally criticised area related to the economy has been taxation, which locals almost proudly proclaim to be the most complicated in the world. It certainly creates plenty of jobs for advisers. Business taxation went through major reforms in 2007, largely to try and rectify a situation where there were so many loopholes that large corporations paid virtually no tax. Income tax is quite high and progressive. Social insurance payments additionally take more than 20 per cent of wages and there's a 5.5 per cent 'solidarity tax' to cover the cost of integrating the former German Democratic Republic. The deductions from an average salary of around €60,000 are likely to amount to around 40 per cent. (For more specific advice on the going rate for your profession, the well respected newspaper *Süddeutsche Zeitung* has a very handy salary comparison mini-site as part of its career section, although of course you'll need to look for the German-language equivalent of your occupation. Visit www.sueddeutsche.de/jobkarriere/erfolggeld/special/126/44082/1 for more information.)

DOING BUSINESS IN GERMANY

Sometimes there's more than a kernel of truth in a stereotype, as you'll probably find out if you do business with Germans. Meetings are generally formal, punctual and stick rigidly to the agenda. You should act accordingly.

Don't attempt to win Germans over with overblown hyperbole. It can be counterproductive and you'll quite possibly be told so as well. Germans can be very blunt.

Although there may be little in the way of small talk at meetings, it can take some time to go through the formalities of the decision-making process. Every detail will be thoroughly checked, so make sure all your paperwork is available and has been translated into German. Decisions, once reached, are final.

WORK AND JOBS

With continuing high unemployment, finding work in Germany isn't easy. Also, it's one of the countries where being a native speaker of English isn't a huge advantage. Most people study English at school and while not *everybody* is fluent, there are enough who are to do you out of a job. That said, if your linguistic skills extend to other, especially non-European, languages you may be in demand as Germany is a major exporter.

Germany traditionally has had a strong system of education, training and apprenticeships. This may mean that skills you've acquired on the job aren't recognised, or the sort of work you've been doing requires specific formal qualifications. Check before you go at the official German government job agency, *die Bundesanstalt für Arbeit* (www.arbeitsagentur.de). It is, of course, in German.

Applications for jobs in Germany follow much the same format as other in countries, with one difference. Your curriculum vitae should be two or three pages long. Copies of appropriate academic certificates should be included, along with references in order of importance. The whole lot should be accompanied by a covering letter and a photograph. Yes, you are expected to include a picture of yourself and many people employ a professional photographer to create the best possible first impression.

It's perfectly acceptable these days to e-mail applications, but you should still take great care to ensure that there are no mistakes in the application and that the layout is perfect. Don't start hassling the human resources department if you haven't heard anything after a week or two. You'll always get a reply from a German organisation eventually.

STARTING A BUSINESS

Anybody who comes from a European Union country has as much right to start a business as a German citizen does. Although it's quite bureaucratic, there are plenty of people who've done it before.

Given the complexity of the country's tax system, it is worth getting an adviser to handle that side of things. You should also be careful how you describe your business activity. Many occupations require registration before you can practise. If, however, you describe yourself as a 'consultant' or 'adviser', you may avoid that bureaucratic trap.

The government is also quite helpful in encouraging people to set up their own businesses, including 'micro-enterprises' which employ just one person. There's even an English language area of the official business start-up portal (www.existenzgruender.de/englisch/index.php). It's also worth approaching the British Chamber of Commerce in Germany (www.bccg.de).

In recent years, the bureaucracy involved in starting a business has been streamlined, especially if you are a registered member of the *Freie Berufe* (liberal professions), such as a tax adviser, doctor or journalist. Then, all you require is a tax number from the tax office. Everybody else setting up a business has to register with the municipality's *Gewerbeamt* (trade office). This is intended to be the 'one-stop shop' that passes your details on to other organisations, but you should still check before you start trading.

You'll need a fair bit of paperwork including:

- ID such as a passport; permits and authorisations from the health office for businesses such as catering
- a craft or trade card recognised across the EU
- proof of occupational accident insurance for you and any staff

You also need to ensure premises have the relevant certificate if a change of use is involved.

All except the smallest businesses have to be listed in the commercial register at the local court. This public register displays information such as the company name, owner, and personally liable shareholders.

There are advantages both in terms of taxation and legal protection to setting up a company. The most popular by far is the private limited liability *Gesellschaft mit beschränkter Haftung* (GmbH). You can set up a GmbH on your own as sole shareholder and managing director, but you must still have share capital of at least €25,000. Otherwise a managing director has to be appointed as the company representative and a notarised agreement drawn up between shareholders.

Although it is possible to transfer the business to a new owner, shares in a GmbH cannot be quoted on the stock exchange. Also, the name of the company has to be derived from either the names of the shareholders or the purpose of the business, so you can't use any of those fashionably meaningless mock Latin names.

Next up in size is the public limited company or *Aktiengesellschaft* (AG) which can have its shares listed on the stock exchange, although it's not compulsory. Again there may be only one shareholder although it has to have a board of directors. Minimum share capital is €50,000.

There are also a number of legal forms of partnership offering different degrees of liability from the unlimited liability of the *offene Handelsgesellschaft* (OHG) to the *Kommanditgesellschaft* (KG) which limits the liability of some partners. These are fairly specialist structures and are not that common.

The GmbH is the powerhouse of the German economy, the *Mittelstand* of small and medium-sized enterprises. The country has relatively few major corporations and they don't dominate in the way they do in, say, the USA or Japan.

That doesn't necessarily make it easy to start a new business. Companies may be relatively small, but they could have been around for generations. There's also a tradition of companies being run by engineers rather than accountants, lawyers or entrepreneurs. A common saying amongst engineers is: 'if it ain't broke, don't fix it'. They don't like to break old relationships either.

ACCOMMODATION AND PROPERTY

The main reason why parts of Germany look so cheap in surveys is because of the price of property, which is among the lowest in Europe. As a result, many investors are looking to buy into a market which is predicted to rise rapidly. Of course, to make the best return you need to buy in the places where property will show the biggest price rises, which isn't much use if you're looking for somewhere to live near where you work.

Most Germans rent their homes. The rental prices can seem high, particularly if for work reasons you're looking for furnished accommodation for a relatively short period. Most rentals are unfurnished and that means without anything, even curtains. And tenants are often expected to redecorate when they move out and to take out insurance as a condition of the lease.

The best place to look for rental property is in the classified section of local newspapers. If you decide to use an estate agent, expect to pay up to two months' rent as commission when the agreement is signed.

You can check whether the price you're being charged is reasonable by consulting the *Mietspiegel*, which lists the cost of rents for each locality. It is displayed in the town hall and landlords can be fined for charging more than 20 per cent above the prevailing level. Generally, tenants are well-protected in Germany.

With property prices generally being a fraction of their British equivalent, buying can seem an attractive proposition. But there are reasons those bargains exist. For a start, the cost of arranging a mortgage is relatively high. More importantly, the German government has discouraged speculation by imposing substantial taxes on properties held for less than ten years.

GREECE

Despite Greece's obvious climatic and cultural attractions, it's never been a major destination for Brits moving abroad. Perhaps the most off-putting factor has been the language, although people argue it's not that difficult once you've learned the alphabet. But that seems to be in the same vein as saying playing the violin is easy once you've mastered the cello.

Some people may also have been put off by the fact that although Greece is the cradle of western civilisation and democracy, it was run by a military junta until the mid-1970s. Mind you, 'the Colonels' gave up power without a struggle when they accepted that they couldn't solve Greece's economic problems either. The country has been democratic ever since.

Today, although Greece might not have the strongest economy in the European Union, it does seem to be improving and EU membership has brought stability. And there are good jobs for English speakers – although a knowledge of Greek obviously helps – in the country's internationally successful industries, which include shipping, banking, telecommunications equipment manufacturing and, of course, tourism.

QUICK FACTS

- **Land area:** 130,800 sq km
- **Population:** 11 million
- **Climate:** It's broadly 'Mediterranean' with hot summers and mild winters. The capital, Athens, and the south of the country can be unpleasantly muggy in August. The winters in the north can be quite cold.
- **Language:** Greek is spoken by 99 per cent of the population
- **Currency:** The euro (£1 = €1.33, January 2008)
- **How long does it take to get there from the UK and are services year round?** Flights from London take approximately four hours. There are regular departures year round from the UK to Athens, but other destinations are less well served outside the summer tourist season.

- **How many British migrants are there and where do they live mostly?** There are about 18,000 UK expats in Greece, mostly in Athens and the main tourist areas.
- **Cost of living:** Overall goods and services cost up to a third less than northern Europe, but Greece is certainly no longer dirt cheap. Prices on the islands tend to be slightly more expensive than the mainland as the result of transport costs and reduced competition.

THE ECONOMY

The Greek economy has always been slightly difficult to measure. Even the government admits that the figures which allowed it to join the eurozone were wrong. More recently Greece has sought to include income from the black economy, including smuggling, prostitution and money laundering in its GDP, partly to reduce the risk of being fined by the EU for failing to control its budget deficit.

It is clear, however, that Greece has been through a period of sustained economic growth, helped by a combination of EU funds, the 2004 Athens Olympics and relaxed consumer credit. The government's challenge is to maintain growth while reducing its budget deficit.

Greece has a well known, large and growing tourist sector representing one-seventh of its GDP and one-sixth of its employment. Perhaps less well known is the fact that Greece has the largest shipping fleet in the world or, more accurately, Greeks own more of the world's ships than any other nationality. (The use of flags of convenience, where ships are registered in a different country from that where they are owned, usually for the purpose of reducing operating costs or avoiding government regulations, means that few people spot this.)

The Greek banking sector has been extremely successful, with growth rates among the best in Europe. It has benefited from being relatively deregulated and because of its stability within the Balkan region. Jobs are often advertised asking for people who speak English and one of the Balkan languages.

Greece also continues to have a successful manufacturing sector, with high-quality food products being the most important export earner. The country also has a flourishing ICT sector, with the production of telecommunications equipment being a particular speciality.

DOING BUSINESS IN GREECE

The word 'nepotism' might come from Latin, but it's a concept that sits happily with Greeks. They prefer to do business with people they know and trust. Who could argue that family doesn't fit this bill?

One effect of this is that there's a good chance it'll be the third meeting with a Greek company before you actually get down to business. The first two meetings will be spent getting to know each other. Negotiations, anyway, tend to move slowly and the Greeks seem to get pleasure out of haggling.

Business relations generally start fairly formally. Being too relaxed, too quickly, may be perceived as discourteous. More importantly, do not challenge somebody's statements publicly or say anything that might impugn the integrity of a colleague. If the meeting suddenly goes quiet you'll know you've overstepped a mark.

The advantage of doing business with Greeks is that once a business relationship is established it's likely to last beyond a single project. At the same time, any contract is likely to be fairly simple because it's based on mutual trust and the realisation that flexibility is necessary.

WORK AND JOBS

Much of the Greek job market may be described as 'informal'. In other words, many posts aren't advertised and interviews are offered on the recommendation of a mutual contact. The obvious lesson here is to build up a business network as quickly as you can.

However the situation is beginning to change, with more advertisements beginning to appear. Some are even in English. Just Jobs (www.justjobs.gr) has jobs that are handled by the executive search and selection arm of international financial services group KPMG. It lists a substantial number of vacancies, not all of which require you to speak Greek. Icap Career (www.icap.gr) is a bilingual executive recruitment site. In Jobs (www.injobs.com) also has business vacancies in Greek and English.

As you might expect, however, the largest number of jobs for English speakers is in language schools. Although it's possible to get work on the islands and in other tourist areas, the best paid posts are in Athens and the other major cities.

You are usually expected to have a university degree to teach at a language school and some insist on a TEFL (Teaching English as a Foreign Language) qualification. The ability to speak Greek is not important. Your aim is to make your students speak English, but if they know you can understand their language it removes part of the incentive.

The work tends to be with children who'll be at 'normal' school in the morning. So your working day will probably be from 3pm until 10pm with contact time of about 25 hours a week. Pay, conditions and the quality of schools varies quite widely. If you have chance it's probably worth visiting more than one.

Many teachers give private one-to-one lessons out of school and this can be quite lucrative, especially if you can find adult students from the business community. It does take time to build up this clientele which usually happens through word of mouth.

Jobs are advertised online at sites such as Anglo-Hellenic (www.anglo-hellenic.com) or TEFL (www.tefl.com) which is not just restricted to Greece. Alternatively you could try visiting schools in person, which is probably the most effective method. The best time to do this is September when they're recruiting for the new school year.

STARTING A BUSINESS IN GREECE

If you dream of being your own boss, taking long lunch breaks under blue Hellenic skies then sipping ouzo on a balmy evening by the Aegean, forget it. Go and buy a lottery ticket instead.

It's not impossible for a foreigner to start a business in Greece, but then people win the lottery every week as well. This may sound odd given that the country has a very high level of self-employment. A 2007 World Bank survey, however, ranked Greece at number 100 in the world for ease of doing business. Another survey from Cushman & Wakefield, an international consultancy, said Athens had the worst business environment of Europe's top 35 cities.

The reality is, according to some entrepreneurs, worse than the World Bank says. It reckons that starting a company requires 15 steps and takes 38 days. 'In reality, each of those 15 steps has other steps and the processing time could be 180 days, unless connections and bribes are used to speed the process,' said one blogger.

Greece has also been very slow to put its official forms and information online. Governments which have embraced the Internet have found this speeds up bureaucratic processes. Greece also has high business taxes which are complex to collect and put an unequal burden on small businesses. There is also a requirement to prove that you have €16,000 in the bank before you start a business, although you can withdraw it all the following day.

Little wonder that, according to the World Bank, it is easier to start a business in such free enterprise power houses as Zimbabwe, the Democratic Republic of Congo or anywhere else in the continent of Europe, not just the EU.

ACCOMMODATION AND PROPERTY

There are almost as many nightmare stories about buying property in Greece as there are in Spain, perhaps because there are similarities in the way the market has developed. In both countries, until relatively recently, property was inherited rather than bought. This has made concepts of ownership sometimes slightly loose.

For many years foreigners couldn't even buy property without resorting to complex legal manoeuvres. It is now relatively straightforward for EU nationals, although the purchase process is anything but cheap. If you are only planning on living and working in Greece for a relatively short time, it is worth considering whether to rent a place to live. Buying is, anyway, not something to jump into without thought.

With over 80 per cent of the population living in homes they own, the rental market is not as large as it is in countries such as Germany. And when you're looking for a place to rent it might feel as if there's a penalty for not being able to understand Greek. There are English-language agents, websites, newspapers and magazines where you can find houses and apartments to rent (such as www.ekathimerini.com or www.athensnews.gr). But many better deals appear in the classified columns of Greek-language papers or, even more likely, from the second cousin of a friend of a friend of a local you've met.

It tends to be far more expensive to rent furnished property and the quality of the furnishings may not be that high. If, however, you are moving to a tourist area, it may be your only initial option. But you may be able to negotiate a reasonable price, particularly outside the holiday season while you look for a longer-term solution.

There are more long-term options outside the resorts and they're generally unfurnished. Be prepared to pay at least two months rent or even more when you move in. Also, make sure that the accommodation really is suitable for a long stay. Rented property is frequently unheated and few places to have been built with winter in mind. Snow, even in Athens, is not unknown.

If you do decide to buy, research is vital. Look online, buy books and, if you possibly can, live for a while in the area where you're planning your property purchase. It's only really by talking to local people that you'll learn which of the area's builders, estate agents and lawyers are good and to be trusted.

Estate agents have to be qualified and are regulated by law. The commission they charge varies between two and five per cent plus tax and is generally included in the purchase price.

Although they're regulated, don't forget they are estate agents who rely on sales to make a living. Many in the tourist areas speak English, but that doesn't mean you should believe every word they say. You may be pressured into making a quick decision because of the 'level of interest' . . . but there's no guarantee that there really is one. If you're planning to work in Greece you may be told that getting a phone line and ADSL installed isn't a problem. You may be told the house is structurally sound, although much of Greece is in an earthquake zone. And you may be told that the person selling the house actually owns it.

The estate agent may well be telling the truth, but verbal confirmation isn't worth the paper it isn't printed on. Get everything checked by your own lawyer, preferably one who has been recommended to you by somebody who has been through the process themselves. Don't pay a deposit or sign any documents until you've taken the opinion of your lawyer. And get the property checked by a structural engineer and a builder as well if the house is 'in some need of improvement'.

Mistakes are expensive even if property prices are relatively low compared with northern Europe. The fees associated with a purchase are up to around 15 per cent. It's easy to be seduced by property which looks perfect on a sunny summer's day, but is cold and damp on a February night. If you decide to sell, you'll either have to take a loss or wait for several years for the increase in the value of the property to cover your initial fees. And that's assuming there are no structural, legal or other problems with its location.

ITALY

Sometimes you get the impression that parts of Italy are so popular with a particular type of Briton that there's hardly room for the Italians. That's why Tuscany is jokingly referred to as 'Chiantishire', a name used even by some local estate agents. In reality, although you might bump into your Notting Hill neighbours buying olive oil in Lucca in the summer, the number of British people living in Italy is relatively small.

The low figure is perhaps largely a reflection of the Italian tourist industry, which hasn't developed the sort of resorts that have major British expat infrastructure of bars, restaurants and shops. Many will find that an attraction. However, finding other employment in the land of the Dolce Vita isn't easy, even for Italians.

QUICK FACTS

- **Land area:** 301,230 square kilometres
- **Population:** 58 million
- **Climate:** The south can be blisteringly hot in summer while the north, rising into the Alps, is very much cooler. The north is also the wettest part of the country, especially in the late autumn months from October through to December.
- **Currency:** The euro (£1 = €1.33, January 2008)
- **How long does it take to get there from the UK and are services year round?** Flight times from London to Rome are a little under three hours. With Milan and Rome in particular being popular weekend break destinations, there are an increasing number of budget and direct flights to these airports. Probably the area most affected by seasonal variations in flight frequency is Sicily.
- **How many British migrants are there?** There are approximately 26,000 British expats in Italy, mostly in the north of the country.

- **Cost of living:** Italy is certainly not a cheap place to live, although it is possible to live fairly frugally if you stick to local produce. Luxury goods and cars seem relatively expensive, but in fact probably don't cost much more than in the UK. Generally, the further south you go, the cheaper it gets. That's especially noticeable with property and rentals, but it's also true generally of things such as meals out.

THE ECONOMY

The Italian economy is faring worse than almost anywhere in Western Europe, with relatively low rates of growth and a high national deficit. Many of the problems are seen as structural.

Italy's industries are mainly in the north and northwest of the country, closest to the heart of Europe as well as to energy and raw materials which are in short supply in Italy. Global competition, however, is plentiful for the country's main manufactured products such as cars, electrical goods, precision engineering and, of course, fashion goods.

The result is what many see as an economy in elegant decline. That said, according to the World Bank, Italy remains the world's seventh largest economy by gross domestic product and there are intermittent signs of recovery, along with a fall in the rate of unemployment. It remains to be seen whether this can be sustained.

DOING BUSINESS IN ITALY

No matter how hard they try, almost every foreigner feels scruffy at an Italian business meeting. That shouldn't stop you trying to dress as immaculately as you can. In Italy, looks matter. This is the country that regards itself, with some justification, as the world capital of fashion.

When you first go into a business meeting it can feel as if you've walked into an argument. It's quite normal in conversation for people to interrupt or raise their voices in order to be heard. That does not mean, however, that everybody is equal. There's great deference for age and seniority. Italian companies and organisations generally have a very rigid hierarchy.

Family and friendship are also highly regarded. A personal recommendation can go a long way, so networking is a valuable exercise (see pp. 168–72). But do make sure that you know whether an event is regarded as social or business: asking about somebody's profession or handing over business cards at a social gathering is regarded as bad manners.

Although the Italian reputation for lack of punctuality is generally undeserved, particularly in the northern cities, don't expect anything to happen fast. Initial appointments are more to do with getting to know you than any proposition you might have to present. Often the most important point is whether you are seen as the sort of person they can do business with.

Finally, don't make the mistake of thinking that the firm handshake, eye contact and sociability of Italians in business means they are a soft touch. On the contrary, driving a hard bargain is part of their culture.

WORK AND JOBS

Finding a job in Italy isn't easy. Unemployment remains high and is worst in the south. At the same time there is very little in the way of state benefits for those without work. On the other hand, those with jobs used to be pretty well protected and there was even a ban on temp agencies until relatively recently.

Most of those restrictions have been removed and an increasing number of Italians now work on contracts rather than getting jobs for life. If you are an EU resident, there should be nothing to prevent you working in Italy, assuming you speak the language. Without fluent Italian, getting work is likely to be very difficult.

However, if you are fluent in both Italian and English, finding a job should be very easy. English is, after all, far more international than Italian and there's a real shortage of people who can speak both languages. The challenge is supporting yourself while improving your language skills.

For people who've moved to Italy under their own steam, teaching English remains the most popular option as a starting point. As is the case generally throughout the world, the best paid jobs are for fully qualified TEFL teachers in the big cities. Along with most industrialised nations, Italy suffers from continuing skills shortages, particularly in IT.

Professionals enjoy the same freedom of movement within the EU as other workers. There is, however, in Italy a particularly strong emphasis on academic achievement. This is partly a reflection of the open-ended nature of Italian higher education, where finishing a degree can take people into their thirties. As a result, proving the equivalence of your British qualifications can be a challenge. You may even have to complete an aptitude test before you can work professionally.

The other side of this emphasis on qualifications is that there are reports of foreign applicants being favoured for jobs in the private sector because they have more work experience than Italians the same age. Either way, it's as well to find out before you leave the UK.

Fortunately, it is now relatively easy to start a job search in Italy from afar. The main business-oriented newspapers such as Milan's *Corriere della Sera* (www.corriere.it/english) and the equivalent of the *Financial Times*, *Il Sole 24 Ore* (www.ilsole24ore.com), for instance, put their recruitment advertising online, as do many professional journals. Of course, applying from the UK means you will not be available for interviews and it's not unknown for organisations to demand handwritten applications so they can be checked by graphologists.

Applying directly to large organisations can be effective, as many jobs are never advertised. Once again, appearance is important. Make sure your CV is well laid out, with your qualifications prominently displayed and that you use good quality paper.

STARTING A BUSINESS

One of the great contradictions of Italy and, in fact, a number of Mediterranean countries is how there can be so many small businesses when starting one seems to be such a bureaucratic nightmare. Why on earth would any potential entrepreneur bother to go through all the necessary hoops?

The answer is that nobody in their right minds now would set up most of the small businesses in Italy. They're generally family-run shoestring operations that only survive because the property they're run from has been inherited and relatives provide the cheap labour. These are businesses that start small and stay small.

There's also another traditional reason for the apparently large number of small businesses – the powerful black economy. This accounts for perhaps a third of Italy's GDP, or as much as half in the poorer south of the country. With low or non-existent unemployment benefit and badly paid civil servants, it's not just illegal immigrants who work cash-in-hand for low pay. Strong labour protection laws and an antipathy to temporary contracts also served to boost the use of untaxed workers.

Although labour laws have been liberalised, making hiring and firing easier, the authorities are seen to be reluctant to clamp down too hard on illegal working for fear of driving large numbers of businesses to the wall. It would be more than foolish to start a business based on the hope that the authorities will continue to ignore the problem, although there are, no doubt, many Brits providing English lessons as part of the 'informal' economy.

Even taking all this into account doesn't explain why over a quarter of the Italian workforce is classified, according to official EU statistics, as self-employed. In fact this doesn't reveal an underlying entrepreneurial spirit, but is the result of the tax status of professionals and people in the entertainment industry. Entrepreneurs generally are not held in the esteem that they are in some other societies such as the US and the UK.

To become self-employed means coping, as you might expect, with a considerable amount of bureaucracy. In most cases you can't just put a sign on your door and tout for custom. Professions have to register with the appropriate body, having first proved their credentials. And the definition of what counts as a profession is rather wider than it is in the UK. My trade as a journalist, for instance, is upgraded to a status it probably doesn't deserve.

Even if your business doesn't count as 'professional', you'll still need to register with the local chamber of commerce. Tax is payable in advance based on previous earnings or, if you're just starting, an estimate of potential earnings. You may also decide to set yourself up as a limited company. Whatever you choose, it really is important to get the right professional advice from a lawyer and accountant.

Perhaps the most straightforward way of tracking down the appropriate experts is through the long-established British Chamber of Commerce in Italy. If it can't find the appropriate expert from among its members, it should be able to point you in the right direction, in English. It's Milan-based but much of its work is done through its website at www.britchamitaly.com.

ACCOMMODATION AND PROPERTY

Despite fast-rising Italian property prices, renting before you buy is still the only sensible option. Mistakes are expensive and you can't really get to know a place until you've seen it all year round. Parts of Notting Hill might decamp to Tuscany for the summer, but they'll be back in London for the winter.

Finding a property to rent isn't difficult, except in the places where you probably want to live, Milan and Rome. That's where most of the jobs are, especially the well paid ones. To find an apartment in either of these cities, realistically you'll probably have to rent before you buy. That means taking a short holiday let while you search for something longer term, and more reasonably priced. This is assuming, of course, you haven't been posted to Rome with a substantial relocation package which means you can afford one of the plentiful serviced apartments mostly occupied by the diplomatic community.

For everybody else, as with any city that has a shortage of suitable property, the best deals come through word of mouth. Let friends, relatives and anybody you meet know you're on the look out. If you've managed to make some contacts through the Internet (see pp. 168–72) ask them too. At the same time, find out when the local papers come out so you can be first in line to check the classified advertisements. Estate agents (*agenzies immobiliares*) rent as well as sell property.

By now you may feel that this is sounding quite difficult for somebody who doesn't speak much Italian. That's because it is hard. Italy remains a country where getting by without a reasonable knowledge of the language isn't easy – although, of course, people do manage.

When you're tramping the city streets, remember the rule of thumb is that the closer to the centre you are, the higher the rents will be. Also, if you manage to find an unfurnished property it'll generally be exactly what it says, without a cooker, fridge or even light fittings. The other thing to be aware of is that prices are always negotiable.

Finding an apartment to rent used to be even more challenging, as many properties were subject to rent controls. Then in 1999 these began to be phased out and replaced by new contracts valid for three or four years depending on whether the rent is negotiated with the landlord who owns the apartment or is part of a national agreement. Contracts have to be registered with the authorities.

Italy is, however, a country of property owners, even if most people do stay at home with their parents up to their thirtieth birthday. The proportion of owner-occupiers is about 70 per cent, not much different from Britain.

Property prices from afar can look very tempting. But that's why you should rent first, to see if that bargain's quite what it seems. The reason rural property can seem so cheap is because the population has migrated to the cities leaving a surplus of empty country homes. If the locals can't find work, there's a good chance you won't be able to either.

Of the cities Rome, Milan and, of course, Venice are the most expensive. Naples is cheapest. But prices vary widely according to neighbourhood and distance from the centre. The main thing, once you've chosen where you want to live, is to do plenty of research. Look at magazines, ask friends, use any source to try and get some idea of how much property actually sells for.

The reason it's so important is that in Italy people always ask more for property than they expect to get. When Italians are buying, they drive a hard bargain. It's expected. Getting an accurate idea of real prices, however, is particularly hard because under-declaring to reduce tax is still very common even though it's illegal. The authorities are trying to clamp down on the practice, revaluing properties and charging owners the difference in tax plus a fine and interest.

The reason people are willing to take the risk is because property taxes in Italy are so high. You should take this into account when deciding what you can afford. Then try and figure out what taxes and fees you will have to pay on top of the purchase price. It is confusing and beyond the scope of this book to go into the detail you really need to know before you take the plunge.

The principal registration tax can be up to ten per cent of the declared value. There are discounts for residents and if it's your first home. New properties are exempt from this tax but subject to IVA (VAT) of up to 20 per cent. There's also a one per cent land registry tax, again with discounts for resident first-home buyers.

Then there are fees for the notary of roughly between €1,500 and €3,000 depending on the price of the property. On top of that the notary will charge 0.25 per cent of the mortgage to put it in the land registry. That's on top of the bank's arrangement fee, administration fee, government mortgage tax and compulsory fire insurance.

Your lawyer, of course, will also want his fee of between one and two per cent of the price. Then there's the estate agent's fee, if you used one, of up to eight per cent, to be divided usually between seller and purchaser. Transfer of utilities also incurs a charge. And of course you may have used the services of a surveyor, architect or other professional.

Even if property prices rise very fast it will take some time to recoup these charges from a sale. That's why it's so important not to make a mistake. Equally, you really do need to find a good lawyer, preferably one who has been recommended by people who have already been through the buying process. Fees vary enormously, as does the quality of service provided. But don't let that make you dispense with legal expertise. Always use a lawyer right from the first document. The idea of signing papers written in a language that's not fully understood, if at all, sounds crazy. But plenty of people do it.

Locals quite often miss out the estate agent and that can make sense. It's often a good way to a bargain and there is no inherent reason why this should cause any difficulties.

Most of the legal problems surrounding property purchase in Italy will be familiar to other Mediterranean buyers. Your lawyer should check that all the planning permissions and licences are in order and registered. Many properties also have several owners through inheritance. They all need to approve the sale. The final thing to ensure is that there are no debts outstanding, including mortgages, utility bills and taxes. These remain with the property and become the responsibility of the new owner.

PORTUGAL

Logically, Portugal should be one of the first places Brits think of moving to. The Anglo-Portuguese alliance is the oldest in the world still to be in existence. It was signed in 1373.

There are other elements of the history of both countries which ought to create similarities. Each had a vast empire, which in Portugal's case only really came to an end in the 1970s. One legacy is that Portuguese is spoken by some 200 million people worldwide, 20 times the population of its country of origin.

The big difference is that Portugal was a dictatorship under Antonio de Oliveira Salazar for a large part of the twentieth century. Since the bloodless 1974 'Revolution of the carnations', the country has been almost *too* democratic, with Lisbon governments only lasting an average of two years.

From an expat point of view, the sluggish economy means there is little to attract people who see working abroad as a career step. There's rather more for those who are looking to downsize, although it's far from being an easy place to start a business.

QUICK FACTS

- **Land area:** 92 million square kilometres
- **Population:** 10,600,000
- **Climate:** There are big differences within Portugal. The south is very dry. The north has cool summers and wet winters. The central area has warm summers and cool, wet winters.
- **Language:** Portuguese
- **Currency:** The euro (£1 = €1.33, January 2008)
- **How long does it take to get there from the UK and are services year round?** Flights from London to Lisbon or Porto are around two and half hours and a few minutes longer to the capital of the Algarve, Faro. Flights to Faro are less frequent in the winter, but are still fairly numerous.

- **How many British migrants are there and where do they live mostly?** There are around 38,000 Brits in Portugal, mostly concentrated in holiday and golfing areas.
- **Cost of living:** Most prices remain lower than in the UK, as do wages. The two are not unrelated. Fresh food, eating out and entertainment generally are cheaper than much of Europe. Second-hand cars, however, are reportedly quite expensive.

THE ECONOMY

By most measures, Portugal holds the unwanted title of 'sick man of Europe'. Its growth in 2006 was the lowest in Europe. In terms of Gross Domestic Product (GDP, which measures the value of goods and services) per head of population, it's been overtaken, according to *The Economist*, by the Czech Republic, Greece, Malta and Slovenia just since 2000.

The European Commission has been very critical of the way public spending in Portugal has been controlled. This is blamed for a budget deficit which reached 6.8 per cent, more than twice that allowed for members of the eurozone under the stability and growth pact.

An added problem since 1974's revolution has been the lack of stable governments. They have lasted on average less than two years. The socialist government under Jose Socrates, however, was elected with a rare absolute majority in 2005. It has introduced a series of measures to reduce the budget deficit, including raising VAT and squeezing public sector pay. The measures appeared to be working.

There remains a stark contrast with the fast-growing economy of Portugal's bigger neighbour on the Iberian peninsula, Spain. For a long time, the latter's growth rates have left it far behind. There is, however, a possibility that Spain's boom, driven by construction and immigration, could prove less sustainable than Portugal's slow development.

DOING BUSINESS IN PORTUGAL

Compared with some Latin countries, the Portuguese are quite conservative and undemonstrative. They certainly don't tend to go in for the stereotypical

Latin gesticulation. Many do, however, show a disdain for deadlines that Brits can find annoying. And being five minutes late for a meeting is regarded as excessively punctual by many Portuguese.

As long as you are extremely polite and formal, you won't go far wrong in dealing with Portuguese business people. Shake hands and make eye contact both when meeting and saying goodbye. Address people as *senhor* or *senhora* followed by their surname. Anybody with a higher university degree is referred to by their honorific title, followed by *doutour* or *doutoura* with or without their surname.

The formality continues into dress. Smart business suits are the norm for men and women. Face-to-face meetings are preferred because they are seen as a better way of developing relationships than over the phone. The need to get to know the people they're dealing with means doing business in Portugal can be slow, at least initially. The compensation is that relationships are viewed as being long term.

Portuguese businesses tend to be fairly hierarchical, with one decision maker. It's obviously important to get to know who that is, although it's usually pretty clear. Along with this conservatism comes a strong respect for seniority. These rules apply to doing business in cities such as the capital, Lisbon, and Porto. Elsewhere (particularly in the Algarve), there may be far less formality, so much so that in those places, you may find that wearing a suit marks you out as a foreigner.

WORK AND JOBS

With the Portuguese economy in such a poor state of repair, it's not surprising that the opportunities for foreigners are limited. Of course, if you are fluent in Portuguese and English that's different. There's a constant demand from organisations that need to do business in English-speaking markets.

For the same reason, there's a continuing call for English teachers. The best-paid jobs are in Lisbon for those with TEFL qualifications. The considerable number of British expats in the Algarve and other tourist areas means competition for these jobs is tougher and the pay lower.

The large tourist sector provides the greatest amount of employment for foreigners. Don't, however, think you're going to earn much more than a subsistence income. The only possible exception is in the property sector, where rare individuals are able to earn substantial amounts in commission. But, even in this industry, most of the people making good money started with a substantial investment of their own.

STARTING A BUSINESS

In a country where most people work for small businesses, you might think the climate would be good for start-ups. Think again. The bureaucracy is a nightmare and it can feel as if everything is being done to prevent foreigners running businesses. That's not true. The sole aim of officials is to protect their own jobs, or so it seems.

All those family businesses might be plentiful, but they're seldom really profitable. Bars, restaurants and shops can often only exist because their premises were inherited so there's no rent or mortgage to pay. Somebody buying into a business is likely to find it hard if not impossible to make ends meet.

The other reason family businesses are so popular is because employing staff is onerous. Labour law very much favours the employee and terminating contracts, which are compulsory, can be very expensive. Many potential employers baulk at the idea of paid leave, social security payments and paid public holidays.

Of course it's not impossible for foreigners to start businesses, just very difficult and time-consuming. The local chamber of commerce or *câmara de comércio* can often help or at least point you in the right direction. Local business people struggle with the bureaucracy too. They may have less sympathy if it becomes clear that you haven't done your homework and thought through the plan for your business. It's surprisingly common.

Part of that homework is finding a skilled English-speaking lawyer and accountant to guide you through the bureaucratic maze. Many expats also employ a *despachante* as a sort of buffer between them and officialdom. Ignorance is no defence if the authorities find you do not have the correct papers or have not paid the correct taxes.

ACCOMMODATION AND PROPERTY

There are huge variations in price whether buying or renting in Portugal. The Algarve and other popular coastal areas, along with the cities of Lisbon and Porto, are generally expensive, whereas inland rural areas can be almost unbelievably cheap. Of course if you're moving to Portugal to work, it's unlikely you'll find a well-paid job anywhere with bargain accommodation.

As with many countries, it makes sense to rent before buying. Many properties which seem attractive in the summer are not adequate for the winter. They often lack sufficient storage space for anybody living in them for more than a few weeks. Also, particularly near resorts, the nature of an area can change quite dramatically between seasons. They may be dead in winter or unbearably crowded in summer. It really takes time to get to know a place.

If you are planning a move to the Algarve and aren't locked into a rigid schedule, winter is often best. Rental for six or even nine months is fairly cheap and it's a good time to get to know the locals. Most rental properties are furnished in these locales.

In Lisbon, Porto and areas generally away from the coast, rentals are more likely to be unfurnished and let long term. Unfortunately there are not many properties available. Many landlords prefer to sell rather than risk having to go through the long and expensive process of evicting anti-social or non-paying tenants. Properties to rent are advertised in Portuguese and English language newspapers and magazines or offered through estate agents, who may also display them on their websites. Although searching online is convenient, the sites aren't always updated that often, so it's best to phone the agent or visit him or her in person.

If you decide to buy, you should find it less risky than in some other countries, but there are still pitfalls, most of which can be avoided by taking the right professional advice. The most useful person to find is an English-speaking lawyer who has been recommended to you by somebody you trust. Also, make sure the estate agent is government registered.

Your lawyer will go through the searches to ensure the title is legal, the property has the correct planning permissions and there are no outstanding bills. In Portugal, debts – including mortgages, taxes and utility bills – remain with the property.

It's not unusual for sellers to expect a certain amount of the purchase price to be paid under the table in cash to avoid capital gains tax. This is, of course, strictly illegal and there are substantial penalties if you're caught. It also means that you stand to pay more tax if you decide to sell later.

One thing to watch out for is taxes and fees, which can add up between 10 and 15 per cent to the price of a property. This is considerably higher than in some other countries.

SPAIN

The continuing love affair between Spain and the Brits remains something of a mystery. It's easy to see why it's the second-most popular destination after Australia for British migrants: there's the scenery, the coast, the food, the people and, above all, the climate. What's harder to see is why the Spanish so willingly accept us.

In a country where it's slightly embarrassing to be seen to be drunk, they seem merely bemused by our binge-drinking compatriots on the *costas*. They also put up with the British way of forming enclaves and stubbornly refusing to learn the language, let alone integrate into the local society. Perhaps it's just part of the general Spanish tolerance for the immigrants who now make up ten per cent of the country's population.

Despite the tolerance, Spain can be an intensely infuriating place to live and work. It's easy to forget how recent much of the economic development is, with most of it dating back just to European Union membership in 1986. Not everything has kept up: bureaucracy, banks, shops and the former monopoly phone company Telefónica have not always discovered American-style customer care. A sales assistant once explained to me how Spanish service works when she'd finished the call on her mobile phone. I was only in the shop for a few minutes, she said, she was stuck there all day.

QUICK FACTS

- **Land area:** 504,842 square kilometres
- **Population:** 45 million
- **Climate:** Spain has perhaps the most varied climate of any country in Western Europe, a fact which sometimes catches immigrants unawares. The northern coastal regions are cool and humid all year. The south is mild in winter, but can be extremely hot in the summer with temperatures reaching 40 degrees Celsius. These are, however, generalisations. There are many microclimates, especially in the south. Inland from Marbella, the

Sierra de Grazalema is the wettest place in Spain with a yearly average of 1887.9 mm. A little to the east is Almeria, which includes Faro de Gata, the driest place in the country with just 91 mm of rain recorded in 2002.

- **Main languages:** Castilian is the official language of Spain. The provinces representing 26 per cent of the population, however, have their own languages which are Catalan (17 per cent), Galician (7 per cent) and Basque (2 per cent). You are unlikely to find many people who speak no Castilian, but regional languages are used for some documents and teaching in some schools is bilingual. Many of the major service companies, such as Telefónica, do provide an English-language service of some sort.
- **Currency:** The euro (£1 = €1.33, January 2008)
- **How long does it take to get there from the UK and are services year round?** It takes between two and four hours to fly from the UK to Spain. Finding the best price can take rather longer. There's a confusing array of full-service and budget airlines serving a wide variety of regional airports in both countries. Service frequencies can vary widely according to season. Places which receive several flights a day during the summer tourist season may only have one or two a week for the rest of the year. This can be a real problem for expats who use Spain as a commuting hub for their work. Airlines are also quick to drop or reduce frequency on routes which are proving unprofitable.
- **How many British migrants are there and where do they live mostly?** As of 2006, there were 274,000 British nationals registered with Spanish town halls, but that figure only tells part of the story. Perhaps three times as many people spend a substantial amount of time in Spain and not just on holiday. There are those who take advantage of broadband Internet and cheap flights to extend their flexible working week to Spain. They probably think it's too complex to try and pay part of their tax in Spain. Other Brits become part of the large black economy that exists in the tourist areas of Andalucía, Alicante, the Balearics and Canary Islands. They work cash-in-hand in bars, restaurants and doing construction work, often for other British expats.

- **Cost of living:** If you're willing to 'go local', prices are generally perhaps 25 per cent lower than in the UK. Some vices such as alcohol and cigarettes are very much cheaper. Domestic utilities such as electricity, gas, water and telephone are somewhat more expensive than Britain. Winter heating bills can be expensive because the Spanish tend not to be very good at insulating their homes. Second-hand cars seem very pricey in comparison with Britain, but petrol and servicing, however, do not cost so much. Also, Spain's equivalent of the MOT, the ITV, is only required every two years and it is not as thorough as the UK test.

THE ECONOMY

The growth of the Spanish economy has been phenomenal, particularly since it joined the European Union (EU) in 1986. It is now the eighth largest economy in the world by GDP according to the World Bank.

Its success in recent years contrasts with other bigger EU economies, particularly those of France and Germany. Spain's growth has been faster and its unemployment lower. There are, however, stark regional disparities. The Basque Autonomous Community and neighbouring region Navarre, along with Madrid, are amongst the most dynamic in the EU with GDPs 125 per cent of the average. In contrast, Extremadura, on the border with Portugal, is just 85 per cent of the average.

There are other concerns. Spain has had relatively high inflation in recent years, fuelled in particular by the booming price of property. This combined with its membership of the eurozone threatens to make its manufactured exports less competitive. It also puts pressure on the mass tourism that has been so important to the country's growth.

Much of the employment that has been created in both service and manufacturing industries has been relatively low-skilled. There are now attempts to raise educational standards, but obviously it will take some time for this to have an impact. Recently there have been complaints that the new graduates lack the skills necessary for employment in the new Spanish economy, leaving them over-educated and underpaid.

DOING BUSINESS IN SPAIN

Family and relationships are central to the Spanish life and that carries into business. The best way to find new clients is to be introduced by somebody they trust. A substantial network is vital for anybody building a business.

Fortunately the Spanish are extremely sociable, although they can also be quite conservative in some ways. You should not, for instance, start using a person's first name until they have initiated it. Likewise, if you speak Spanish, using the informal *tu* should be left until it is clear that this is what's expected.

Incidentally, you may be aware that what we call 'Spanish', or more properly Castilian, is only one of the languages of the country. In Barcelona, for instance, Catalan is the official language. Although using a few words of Catalan in the right setting may impress your hosts, it's not vital. In fact, given the rapid growth of Barcelona, there's a reasonable chance the business person is from outside Catalonia and knows no more than you.

Wherever you are, you'll realise the Spanish are far more tactile than the British. For men, shaking hands is the minimum, even if you just come across an acquaintance in passing, and hugging is quite common. Women are kissed on both cheeks, left first, even in formal situations. The process is repeated when saying goodbye, which means leaving a meeting can be quite time-consuming.

WORK AND JOBS

Although there are large numbers of British people working in Spain, the majority are in low-paid service jobs doing work related to the tourist industry. The construction industry boom initially employed a large number of British trades people, but that has declined as a result of competition from workers from other countries.

There is continuing demand for native-speaking English teachers. The majority of language schools are small and many don't require specific qualifications. The work is not well paid and many Brits teach individuals or classes through the winter then work in the tourist industry in the summer. The larger language schools which do demand qualifications are concentrated more in the larger cities, particularly Madrid and Barcelona.

Most professional and managerial jobs require a high proficiency in Spanish. One of the exceptions is IT, in areas such as programming. In Madrid, for instance, there is an ongoing demand for computer specialists to service its increasingly important role as a financial centre, based partly on its strong traditional links with Latin America. Barcelona is the media centre of Spain. Web experts are always required. Even where jobs are plentiful, a reasonable fluency in Spanish is extremely useful. If nothing else, it could give you an advantage over the increasing number of well-qualified workers coming to Spain from the new EU countries.

STARTING A BUSINESS

Compared with many European countries, self-employment is a reasonably straightforward option, although you would be foolish not to take professional advice. Fortunately that's generally cheaper than it is in the UK.

As an *autónomo*, you have to register with both the Spanish tax office (Agencia Tributaria – www.aeat.es) and the department of social security. You'll probably then have to complete a quarterly return for VAT (IVA in Spain) and an annual tax return. Many locals and foreigners use an accountant to complete the forms, although they're not terribly complicated.

What can be quite difficult for people starting a business is that the minimum social security payment can seem quite high compared with the UK, especially as rates of pay are generally lower. The answer is to budget for these payments for at least the first six months. Be prepared to earn a lot less than you expect.

Professionals planning to practise in Spain have to register with appropriate bodies to get their qualifications recognised. There isn't, however, the sort of legal pressure to do this that there is, for instance, in France. If there isn't a suitable organisation for your line of work you don't have to try and find one.

There may be advantages to setting up a limited company if only, as in Britain, to protect yourself from personal liability. There are, however, additional financial reporting requirements which may mean it's not worth it. As ever, you should consult a professional and, preferably, find somebody who is in approximately the same position as you to talk it through with.

ACCOMMODATION AND PROPERTY

Rents are usually lower than in the UK with greater security for tenants. The difficult part is finding somewhere to rent in the first place. There are websites, but few are particularly reliable or frequently updated. You really need to be on the spot to get a good deal.

The best places to look for the long-term rentals (known as *viviendas*) are local newspapers, estate agents and word of mouth. It does help if you speak the language or can find somebody to act as an interpreter. Renting through an English-speaking agent may be more convenient, but it's also usually more expensive than using somebody truly local.

Remember, prices are always negotiable and there will also be costs that you hadn't expected. You'll be asked for a month or two's rent as a deposit and if you use an agent they'll expect a month's rent as commission. And 'agent' can be a fairly vague term, covering anybody except usually the person you're renting from.

Generally, 'rent before you buy' is a good motto to stick to in most countries, but perhaps more so in Spain. The polite way of describing the property sales system is 'loosely regulated'. Anybody can describe themselves as an estate agent and take their five per cent commission. A common pattern is for a property to be advertised in the local paper. The seller is then besieged by an army of estate agents and possibly the odd potential purchaser. It stands to reason that if you're in the area with access to the local paper, you can deal direct with the seller without anybody having to pay commission. And, of course, many sales don't even touch the newspapers and rely on word of mouth. Those bargains go to people who live locally.

Everybody seems to have heard a horror story about Spanish property purchases. It's certainly the case that some of these disasters could have been avoided with a little local knowledge and a modicum of common sense.

Planning laws in Spain can seem arbitrary or even corrupt. Indeed, there are a string of high profile cases going through the courts at the time of writing. It's also common to build without the correct permissions in the hope that the work will be legalised after a few years if nobody complains.

The visitor who comes on a fortnight's holiday, sees a flat they like and puts down a deposit won't suspect anything might be wrong. If you *live* in a place, however, you'll find the locals and local expats will have a pretty good idea of which properties may be a bit dodgy.

The same people can also probably point you in the direction of a good lawyer, one who is completely independent from your estate agent or property developer. Some locals will have been through the purchase process themselves and will probably know which legal professional can hold your hand and tell you when you should worry and when you shouldn't.

Once you've found a place you want to buy, you should contact your lawyer immediately. Don't sign anything without asking legal advice. You will probably be under pressure to move quickly, especially if an estate agent is involved. Acting too fast is the way to make expensive mistakes. Anyway, the price is always negotiable and that takes time.

Before you pay any deposit, there are a series of checks you and your lawyer should make. These include: what debts including mortgages there are against the property; that it is properly described in the title deeds; that new buildings and improvements to old ones, such as the addition of extensions and swimming pools, have the appropriate planning permission; there are no local taxes outstanding; utility bills are up to date; community charges for maintenance have been paid and so on. It's important to remember that debts belong to the property so, without care, you could end up paying the original owner's bills.

When buying a property off-plan, you may pay a small deposit of a few thousand euros to reserve your choice for 30 days or so. More generally you'll then pay a deposit of ten per cent of the agreed purchase price, and you'll lose this if you back out. If the *vendor* backs out, he or she will pay you double your deposit.

The final stage of what most people feel is an intensely nerve-wracking process takes place in the notary's office with your lawyer, bank manager and the vendor, probably with their lawyer and bank manager. You'll need your passport and 'NIE', which is an identification number issued to foreigners through the police station or the Spanish embassy and consulates in the UK. There'll be a series of deeds to sign.

At the end of the official process, most of the representatives will leave. That's when an envelope of cash is handed to the vendor. This is the undeclared money which is still part of many property deals, especially in rural areas. It is illegal and really you should avoid making such payments, but that may be easier said than done.

AUSTRALIA

It surprises some people that Australia, a country on the other side of the world, is still far more popular than anywhere in Europe as a destination for Brits moving abroad to live. The main thing this reflects, perhaps, is the power of language. By and large we lack the linguistic skills to compete for work in neighbouring European states, despite the freedom of movement granted to us as EU members.

Australia, along with New Zealand and Canada, has a seemingly insatiable demand for English-speaking skilled workers. But, before you jump on the next Quantas jet to a new life down under, you really need to do your homework. The climate isn't all 'Neighbours' sunshine. And work qualifications are perhaps more rigidly scrutinised than in any other country in the world.

QUICK FACTS

- **Land area:** 7,682 million square kilometres
- **Population:** 20.2 million
- **Climate:** Anybody who has spent their life in a nice temperate climate is liable to find the Australian weather something of a shock. Much of the interior is desert. People, however, live mostly on the coast, a quarter of which is tropical. This can be unpleasantly hot, humid and stormy. In the temperate zones, which are the most heavily populated, it can rain for days.
- **Main language:** English
- **Currency:** Australian dollar (£1 = Au$2.20, January 2008)
- **How long does it take to get there and are the services year round?** A flight from London to Sydney is 23 hours 30 minutes. Adelaide takes about an hour longer and Darwin a couple of hours less.
- **How many British migrants are there?** There are 1.3 million Brits in Australia.
- **Cost of living:** Australia used to have a reputation for being cheap, but Sydney's now one of the most expensive cities in the world to live, largely

due to its high rents and property prices. Nowhere else is quite as expensive as Sydney, but the strength of the Aussie dollar has pushed up the cost of anything imported. It's also a country where salaries are fairly low and taxes are high.

THE ECONOMY

The Australian economy has a slightly unusual balance, although it's pretty stable. Mining and agriculture only account for eight per cent of GDP and yet they represent two thirds of exports. This reflects the lack of a substantial manufactured export sector.

This could make the economy vulnerable to a downturn in commodity prices, but at the moment the country is benefiting from the boom in nearby China which has substantial contracts for commodities such as minerals and liquefied natural gas. This has increased the government's income from company taxes.

Recently the national government has focused on the development of tourism, education and technology. It funds scientific research and development through universities and through joint ventures between the public and private sectors called Cooperative Research Centres.

Overall, the economy is pretty successful with a GDP per head better than countries such as France and Germany, although behind the UK and USA.

DOING BUSINESS IN AUSTRALIA

In a country that values informality so highly, mentioning 'business etiquette' seems almost perverse. But it's as easy to annoy Australians as any other nationality.

Try puffing yourself up with exaggerated claims as part of a presentation and you'll have a queue of Aussies wanting to take you down a peg or two. They'll also expect you to get straight to the point without getting bogged down in too much detail. It's not a culture which is based on bargaining either. Of course, anything's negotiable, but you should start from a point that seems realistic.

While taking yourself too seriously might be seen as the ultimate crime, virtues such as punctuality are valued as much as they are in any other business culture. And while a sense of humour might be valued highly, don't laugh at the bloke wearing Bermuda shorts with a shirt and tie in Brisbane. It's normal business attire.

JOBS AND VISAS

For a number of years Australia has been struggling to cope with major skills shortages across a number of industries and professions. The government even lists the shortages in a regularly updated Migration Occupations in Demand List which you'll find on the official visas and immigration website (www.immi.gov.au). For the right people, immigration is easier than it has been for a long time. But 'easier' is a relative term.

Anybody who isn't from New Zealand needs a visa to visit or work in Australia. There are a bewildering number of classes and sub-classes of temporary and permanent work visas. For a family the application process will probably cost about £2,000 before you start thinking about paying for the move. To get a visa from London, which is faster than most places, will probably take about four months.

The Australian Migration Programme has three streams. The rules for each are, in general terms:

- Skill – migrants must satisfy a point test, have particular work skills, be nominated by particular employers, have other links to Australia or have successful business skills and/or significant capital to bring to Australia to establish a business of benefit to the country.
- Family – selected on the basis of the family relationship to a sponsor in Australia – essentially spouses, fiancés, dependent children and parents who meet the 'balance of family' test (a test designed to give an indication of how strong the parents' family links are with Australia compared with other countries).
- Special Eligibility – covers former residents who had not acquired Australian citizenship and are seeking to return to Australia as permanent residents.

There's also a humanitarian programme for refugees and humanitarian cases.

There's a need for almost every type of qualified professional and people skilled in trades. Visas are available fairly readily to people who are qualified, have been working in their occupation for at least three years and are aged under 45. But before you rush to start a new life in the sun, you should be aware that there are catches.

In general salaries are lower than in Britain. The cost of living is, however, not that much less. There may also be fewer opportunities for promotion and career development than in the UK.

A further problem has been that a visa doesn't guarantee a job. In fact ending up with the wrong sort of visa can be a nightmare. Even with the right paperwork, many new migrants complain that the process of getting their skills and qualifications recognised is time-consuming and bureaucratic, often duplicating the requirements for the visa. It's not even necessarily a once-in-a-lifetime experience, as each state has different requirements.

The process can take more than a year after arrival in Australia. New migrants with trade skills frequently have to prove their abilities at school over several months then have them recognised by the appropriate trade body. A large number of people simply give up and return to the UK.

The so-called 'General Skilled Migration' (GSM) visa programme has been going through a review, which led to substantial changes in September 2007. The key difference is a greater emphasis on English language skills. Foreign nationals from the UK, US, Canada, Ireland and New Zealand are deemed automatically to meet the threshold level of English language proficiency. Labor's 2007 general election victory may bring more changes.

Work visas are granted on a points basis, with the main emphasis being on the occupation of the applicant. The website for the Australian Government Department of Immigration and Citizenship has links to the skilled occupation lists for the various states. A native English speaker under 45 with qualifications and experience in one of this huge list of occupations in demand should have no problem getting a visa.

You can also apply for jobs in Australia before you get a visa. The main stipulation is that the employer hasn't been able to fill vacancy with an

Australian citizen. You'll still have to meet the other criteria in order to be admitted and the process will still take several months.

There's also a demand for people who can run their own businesses and have a proven track record as an owner, executive or investor. Most come on a temporary four-year visa.

The process of immigration is complicated, as it is in any country. However there is no shortage of information, much the opposite. The laws are constantly being revised, so do make sure you study the websites for the Australian government nationally and the individual states. Their information is up to date and, generally, it's not too impenetrable.

Dealing with any bureaucracy, though, inevitably brings its problems. Applicants do make mistakes when filling in forms and there's no shortage of horror stories from people who have been wrongly rejected or ended up with inappropriate visas.

Many people, therefore, decide to use a migration agent, although it's not strictly necessary. Applications will not be decided any sooner nor will it affect the outcome, except to the extent that the forms should have been filled in properly. However, if you do not feel confident in lodging an application, or if your case is complex, you may wish to use a migration agent to help you.

In Australia, migration agents have to be registered with the Migration Agents Registration Authority (MARA) in order to provide immigration assistance services. Although registration obviously can't be enforced internationally, it would be a mistake to use anybody without MARA certification. Since the end of 2006 this has been particularly true, as registered agents inside and outside Australia may now certify copies of original documents that relate to visa applications.

Agents can also:

- advise you on the visa that may best suit you
- tell you the documents you will need to submit with your application
- help you fill out the application form
- submit the application for you
- communicate with the department on your behalf

There are some people who suggest that anybody considering a move to Australia within the next few years should apply for a visa now while they are relatively easy to get hold of. Visas are currently valid for five years and the period can be extended for a further five years. Do ensure that this remains the case, as applying for a visa is expensive in terms of both time and money.

STARTING A BUSINESS

To start a business in the UK is a real challenge; to attempt it half way round the world may sound like the ultimate folly, but people do manage it. And it's not as difficult as it might be in some other places. The business system is based on British law and it's transacted in English – or at least the lawyer's equivalent of the language.

The biggest bureaucratic challenge is the complexity of tax law. Not employing a professional to provide advice in this area could be a very expensive mistake. You should also ensure that you go through all the same processes of market research and due diligence that you would when starting a business in Britain, even if geography makes it more difficult.

In fact it is well worth considering buying a going concern rather than starting a new business from scratch. There are business brokers who specialise in this area and who should help to prevent any really expensive mistakes.

Once you've got the finance in place, sorted your cash flow analysis and written your business plan, you can start to consider the structure for the business. Most of the entities are much the same as in the UK.

Sole trader is the most straightforward. You can use your own name without registering it. The paperwork is limited and you keep the profits. The main downside is that you're personally responsible for all debts.

A partnership establishes joint ownership of a business. Everything is handled equally unless you draw up an agreement to say otherwise. You have to file a partnership return to the tax office.

A limited company exists as a separate entity from its shareholders, which means the owners' assets can't be touched to cover debts. There may be tax advantages and it could be easier to gain investment. The paperwork and regulation is, however, quite onerous in comparison with partnership or sole trader status.

A trust is slightly different from anything that exists in Britain, but is quite popular in Australia. Usually the assets of the trust are owned by a company, the trustee, although this can be an individual. Currently it has tax advantages although rules may change.

Check whether you need to register your business name and if there are any permits or licences required. There probably will be, as there are hundreds of permits associated with different types of business. Confirm you meet your insurance liabilities as well. For instance, workers' compensation insurance is mandatory for directors and employees.

The best starting point for further information is the Australian government's business information gateway website www.business.gov.au. And do visit the forums on the various international and Australian expat websites. You'll find no shortage of people willing to offer advice.

PROPERTY AND ACCOMMODATION

As when moving to any new country, it makes sense to rent before you buy. This can seem costly, especially in somewhere such as Sydney with a shortage of property to let, but it's cheaper than making an expensive mistake by buying the wrong home.

Most properties are let by agents whose main job seems to be to vet tenants, so it's worth ensuring you're not too scruffy if you go to see them. Most of them also have websites, although they may not be updated that regularly or include everything they've got on their books. Get in touch and ask.

When you find a place you'll probably be charged a fee equal to two weeks rent on a one-year lease, which is the legal maximum. You'll also have to pay a month's rent in advance, a deposit for electricity and gas, plus a fee for drawing up the lease document.

The other money you'll have to pay up front is for the deposit or 'bond' as it's called in Australia. This is held by the 'Rental Bond Board' along with a copy of the inspection report for the property.

The main problem faced by new immigrants looking to buy property is the absence of a local credit history. Many Australian mortgage brokers or banks are often not sure how to deal with people who have a large sum of cash, but don't tick the boxes in the list from head office. It's worth approaching immigration specialists, such as Aussie Migrant (www.aussiemigrant.com), who won't regard you as odd for not having a year's worth of Aussie pay slips.

Spending time in the area where you are planning to buy will also give you an idea of the real value of local property. It may be possible to offer well under the asking price, especially if the market is flat.

A higher proportion of properties are sold by auction in Australia than in the UK. They represent up to a third of sales in some areas. There are bargains, but there aren't the cooling-off rights that exist when you buy a home by more conventional means. You can use an estate agent to find a place and bid for it.

Self build is very popular in much of Australia, although it might be a little adventurous if it's your first home in the country. There's no shortage of land, although the same can't be said for builders. Along with the usual bureaucratic hassles, such as the six months or so spent gaining planning permission, there never seems to be enough skilled tradespeople or professionals such as architects. Be prepared for it to take a couple of years from the time you buy your land to moving into your dream home.

Renovation can be similarly slow, with what can seem fairly limited structural alterations requiring planning permission. Do get the house surveyed and checked by a pest inspector even if it's not a legal requirement. Termites are a problem in parts of Australia.

The process of purchasing and conveyancing is much the same as it is in England and Wales. It includes carrying out searches to ensure that the title deeds are in order and that there aren't any planned developments that would affect the property. Levels of taxation and stamp duty vary from state to state.

And, just as in England and Wales, you can be gazumped, especially if property prices are rising. After you've paid your holding deposit to show you're interested, another purchaser can come in and offer more than you. It happens.

CANADA

Canada is often portrayed as a sort of 'US Lite', and assumed to be lacking the dynamism, excitement and dreams of its more dominant neighbour. But then neither does it have the inequalities, violence and other social problems of the US of A. It's also crying out for skilled workers.

With a conscious political will to attract immigrants who are able to contribute to the economy, it's generally perceived as a good place for foreigners. The only common expat complaint is that that salaries aren't high enough to make a fortune in Canada to take back to your country of birth. They are enough, however, to enjoy a good standard of living in Canada.

QUICK FACTS

- **Land area:** 9,984,670 square kilometres
- **Population:** 33 million
- **Climate:** There are huge variations in Canadian weather. Along the Arctic Circle, the temperature stays below freezing for more than half the year. On the south-western coast, meanwhile, summer temperatures regularly pass 30 degrees Celsius with high humidity as well. The temperatures still drop below zero in winter, though.
- **Main languages:** English and French are both official languages.
- **Currency:** Canadian dollar (£1 = Can$1.98, January 2008)
- **How long does it take to get there from the UK?** Flights from London to Calgary take nine hours; to Halifax is seven hours; to Montréal is seven hours 20 minutes; to Toronto is eight hours and to Vancouver is nine hours 45 minutes.
- **How many British migrants are there?** There 603,000 Brits in Canada spread throughout the country.
- **Cost of living:** The biggest difference compared with the neighbouring USA is in healthcare. In Canada, the system is funded through taxes so the

difficulties and costs of insurance don't exist, nor are citizens bankrupted if they fall ill. Otherwise prices for most goods and services seem cheaper than in the UK. This includes food, eating out, driving, utilities and housing.

THE ECONOMY

Canada is the world's second largest country by area, after Russia. The land mass includes enormous quantities of natural resources including timber, gold, nickel, uranium, gas and oil. The country has the world's second-largest oil reserves and plentiful sources of hydro-electric power. Unusually for an advanced nation, it is a net exporter of energy, mostly to the USA.

What has always been missing is a large manufacturing sector. This meant that Canada didn't go through the painful changes that other countries suffered when their manufacturing base shifted to lower wage economies. Really the only major manufacturing carried out in Canada is of motor vehicles. Most of the plants are branches of US or Japanese companies.

The service sector is huge. Retailing is the biggest employer, followed by business services, education and health. The country also has an important IT industry. In addition, it produces movies and television programmes for global consumption. Tourism is of growing importance as well, although the weakness of the US dollar has had a negative impact.

DOING BUSINESS IN CANADA

The main thing to be aware of is that Canadians are divided into English-speaking Anglophones and French-speaking Francophones. The difference has social and, more importantly, legal ramifications. Canada is officially bilingual. In Quebec province, which has the biggest concentration of French speakers, all promotional material and other documents must be offered with a full French translation. Companies doing business across Canada may also expect bilingual documentation. It certainly does no harm to apply this to your business cards.

Otherwise, doing business with Canadians is not that different from in Britain. The high-pressure sales pitches that sometimes work across the border are likely to be ineffective. Likewise, Canadians are much less inclined to wear their flag on their sleeve. The chances are that your meeting will start in the same way as it would in the UK, with a chat about the weather.

JOBS AND VISAS

For a number of years Canada has had a deliberate policy of creating a high per-capita level of immigration, based on the theory that it results in a net gain to the economy. Whether this is effective is still a subject for debate, but it does mean that if you have a skill which is in short supply, getting work in, and admission to, Canada is fairly straightforward.

And most skills *are* in short supply: a global survey in 2006 by the employment services company Manpower showed that only Mexico had greater problems finding staff. Two-thirds of employers in Canada reported having difficulty filling positions due to a lack of suitable talent. That compares with 40 per cent of employers worldwide. The survey covered 33,000 employers across 23 countries and regions.

In Canada, the survey found the positions employers were having the most difficulty in filling are for sales representatives, followed in order by customer service representatives, engineers, drivers, mechanics, labourers, chefs or cooks, electricians, skilled trades and nurses. The country's growing IT sector is also facing major recruitment problems, with shortages across the board.

Partly in order to resolve this crisis, Canada accepts around 200,000 new residents each year, but that doesn't mean the permanent visa application process is simple. In common with most countries, Canada's immigration policy is constantly being modified. (Visit www.entercanada.ca/canadaimmigration.htm to keep up to speed.)

The equivalent of the US Green Card in Canada is the Immigration (Permanent Resident) Visa, which allows you to live and work anywhere in Canada. To retain it you must be in Canada for the equivalent in days of two years in five and you're not allowed to vote. Apart from that, the visa confers just about all the same privileges as citizenship and you can apply for that after three years.

Probably the most relevant form of application for readers of this book is as a skilled worker. This is based on six criteria with a theoretical maximum score of 100. The combined qualifying level is 67, based on:

1. **education:** maximum 25 points.
2. **language skills:** maximum 24 points.
3. **experience:** maximum 21 points.
4. **age:** maximum 10 points.
5. **arranged employment:** maximum 10 points
6. **adaptability:** maximum 10 points

Unfortunately, scoring 80 points won't absolutely guarantee entry, but at least you'll have an idea of whether it's worth pursuing a visa. (There are a number of websites which include enough detail to estimate a personal total, such as www.skillclear.co.uk/canada/canada-skilled-worker-points-calculator-1.asp or www.global-emigration.com/canada/canadian-skilled-visa-points-calculator.asp. The authorities will also take into account the state of the job market, whether an applicant has a criminal record and other factors before making a decision.

Bilingual Quebec province has slightly different criteria, with more emphasis on proficiency in French, family characteristics and financial self-sufficiency. Any applicant without sufficient funds will be automatically rejected.

Across the country, business immigration is intended to bring in individuals who will help to develop Canada's economy. Applicants are expected to have considerable business and management experience and a fairly high net worth.

1. Investors in 2007 were expected to be worth personally at least CAD $800,000 (£400,000) and be willing to make a secured investment of CAD $400,000.

2. Entrepreneurs in 2007 were expected to have a net worth of at least CAD $300,000 and show they are capable of starting, buying or

investing in a business that would create or maintain jobs in Canada.

3. 'Self-employed' is the other category of business immigrant and it doesn't necessarily mean exactly what you'd expect. It's actually aimed at professional sports people, artists and actors who can make a significant contribution to the economy or the cultural and artistic life of Canada. Strangely, this category also includes farmers.

Family class sponsorship is open to people with a close relative who is already a citizen. Almost a third of people emigrating to Canada follow the family route. It's a serious commitment with a legal obligation to maintain sponsorship for up to ten years.

If you already have a place in mind that you'd like to move to, you can apply directly through the province's immigration office. Usually this means that you, as the applicant, have been offered a job which will economically benefit the province. The local government can then nominate the individual applying through the federal office.

A family of four with two dependent children aged under 22, as of 2007, will pay around CAD $2,000 in fees. On top of this you'll be expected to pay for medical examination and possibly for legal notarisation of professional documents.

STARTING A BUSINESS IN CANADA

It may seem odd that Canada isn't the first choice for Brits wanting to set up on their own. After all, according to the World Bank, in 2007 Canada rated as the second-easiest place in the world to start a business, beaten only by Australia. It's also largely English-speaking and has the enormous market of the USA on its doorstep.

The reasons for this apparent anomaly are varied, but it mainly comes down to the type of business that people aspire to run. Generally, British dreams of escaping from the nine-to-five are made up of what 'real' entrepreneurs describe, somewhat disparagingly, as 'lifestyle businesses'. These can support an individual or a family financially, but they're not designed for growth. It's unlikely, for instance, that anybody seriously expects their B&B to develop into a chain of hotels. People also tailor their dreams for expediency. If it were easier to get a salaried job in the South of France or Costa del Sol, I'm sure far less Brits would be trying to open bars there.

Canada, however, has no shortage of jobs for skilled English-speakers. That means the logical path for anybody who meets the visa criteria mentioned earlier is to find employment first and then think about starting a business. To try and set everything up from across the Atlantic is likely to be both difficult and unnecessary. It's hard enough to launch a successful business wherever you are.

In Canada, the initial bureaucracy is anyway very straightforward and quick. All the forms necessary can be completed online. In the average industrialised country, it takes six steps and 15 days to launch a business. In Canada, there are just two steps which take an average of eight days to complete.

That's the good news. The country isn't rated so favourably by the World Bank in other areas such as registering property; dealing with licences; paying taxes; importing and exporting. Difficulties in those areas drag Canada down the business-friendly ratings.

It's worth bearing in mind that Canada is a strongly federal country which means, amongst other things, that the regional red tape varies enormously as do the levels of federal, provincial and local taxation. In one jurisdiction, according to Garth Whyte, executive vice-president of the Canadian Federation of Independent Business, you need up to 120 permits to run a B&B.

Despite these challenges, and nobody in business ever complains about a lack of taxation or bureaucracy, Canada is still one of the best countries in the world to run a business. And the big advantage it has compared with its big neighbour is its healthcare system. You won't lose your life savings if you fall ill.

There is also a plenty of government support and advice for would-be business people. Each state has its own website which can be reached the national portal (www.canadabusiness.ca). Or try this self-explanatory site: www.beyourownboss.org.

PROPERTY AND ACCOMMODATION

When you arrive in Canada, you'll probably start by renting furnished accommodation. It's expensive but leases are short, properties are easy to find on the Internet and it's a useful stopgap until you find something longer term.

Your best sources for rental properties are Craig's List (www.craigslist.org), which dominates property classified advertising throughout much of North America; classified sections of local newspapers online and agencies. Try searching for 'rental agencies' or 'rental suites' in the area where you want to live.

Generally the rental market in Canada is very highly regulated compared with many countries. Although this means you should be pretty well-protected as a tenant against unfair rent increases and eviction, there is a possible downside. Some people (notably landlords) say over-protection is leading to a shortage of rental property, a situation which is exacerbated by the loss of 'better tenants' who are opting to buy rather than rent.

The legislation covering property rental varies from state to state, so you'll need to check the specifics when you decide on your location. The best general source of information for both buying and renting is the Canada Mortgage and Housing Corporation (www.cmhc-schl.gc.ca).

Most tenancy agreements run for a year initially, and then roll over onto a month by month basis. Make sure you know what's included: the rent for one apartment might appear cheaper because heat and other utilities aren't incorporated, or there may be an additional charge for parking.

In most states, rent cannot be increased more than once annually and then only by a fixed amount over inflation. There's usually arbitration service in case of disagreements between landlords and tenants. At the start of an agreement, the landlord will ask for a security deposit which often can't be more than half a month's rent. There's joint inspection by landlord and tenant before the deposit is paid. It's repaid at the end of an agreement, with interest.

Buying a property is generally much more straightforward than in Britain. For a start, all properties for sale through 'realtors' (or 'estate agents' as they would be in the UK) are available on the searchable Multiple Listings Systems website (www.mls.ca).

Realtors are all officially licensed and have access to more MLS information such as the sales history of a property. The idea is that you engage a realtor who will show you the properties available that meet your criteria. They'll advise you on how much to offer and other clauses you may want to include.

The seller may accept your offer or ask for sealed bids by a certain date. If your offer is accepted, you generally have a 'cooling off' period of a few days in order to arrange finance, a building inspection and land registry searches. Then you pay a deposit and sign a binding contract. And that's it apart from the closing costs - you can't be gazumped.

There are, of course, various fees and taxes to be paid according to the state where you're buying. These could include: Property Transfer Tax, notary fees, survey, mortgage application fee, appraisal fee for the lender, building inspection fee if you want to check for defects, property tax which may already have been paid by the owner, Goods and Services Tax for new homes and 'strata fees' if you're buying a condominium. The vendor pays the realtor.

CHINA AND HONG KONG

PEOPLE'S REPUBLIC OF CHINA

For centuries, mainland China was effectively closed to foreigners. Even when it began to open up to tourism, it was only through closely-monitored trips to the main attractions. Then in the 1980s, the giant collective farms were dismantled and private enterprise was legalised. It also joined the World Trade Organization which opened up not only other markets, but its own.

The sleeping giant awoke. The economy of the world's most populous market began its long economic boom. Major businesses felt they couldn't be left out, and new opportunities appeared for anybody wanting to experience a huge country with a completely different culture. Instead of being part of a tour group, you could actually live, work and really begin to learn about China and its people. Of course, this massive upheaval isn't painless. The traditions which stretch back thousands of years don't include private enterprise. There is often a 'Wild West' element to doing business and protecting the environment has seldom been a priority. The pollution in many places is horrendous.

There's probably nowhere more exciting to live and work in the world at the moment than China. But nobody said it was going to be easy.

QUICK FACTS

- **Land area:** 9,596,960 square kilometres
- **Population:** 1.3 billion
- **Climate:** There are enormous variations in climate, but generally it's characterised by dry seasons and monsoons. Beijing, for example, has summer temperatures which frequently hit 38 degrees Celsius (100

degrees Fahrenheit) during the rainy season. In the winter, temperatures drop as low as minus 20 degrees Celsius.

- **Languages:** Standard Mandarin is the official language, although the family of Chinese includes between six and twelve often mutually unintelligible languages and dialects.
- **Currency:** Yuan Renminbi (£1 = 14.20 yuan, January 2008)
- **How long does it take to get there from the UK?** Flights from London to Beijing take approximately 10 hours. To Shanghai is roughly 11 hours.
- **How many British migrants are there?** Approximately 36,000.
- **Cost of living:** Beijing and Shanghai generally register among the world's top 20 most expensive cities. That only tells a tiny part of the story, though. Pay and living standards for the Chinese are still generally much lower than the West. The big cities do offer plenty of ways to spend all you can earn (and more), but equally you can live very well on a foreign salary. The biggest expense is likely to be accommodation.

THE ECONOMY

Many countries would envy China's economic problems. With growth projected to continue at round about ten per cent and the world's third-largest gross domestic product (GDP), the greatest threats come from overheating (growing too quickly, in other words) and skills shortages. These may slow growth a little, but nobody expects it to stop or go into reverse.

The economic ideology is described as 'socialism with Chinese characteristics'. In practice, this means 70 per cent of the GDP is in the private sector while the public sector controls heavy industry, utilities and energy. The heavy-handed control of the economy by the Communist Party has gradually been loosened with small-scale local enterprise and foreign investment being encouraged. This is still very much focused on manufacturing, but multinationals are beginning to shift some of their research and development to China as well.

DOING BUSINESS IN CHINA

Business etiquette, and Chinese culture as a whole, is such a minefield that perhaps the best any Westerner can hope is that any faux pas committed are not too horrendous. The key, and most difficult, thing to understand is the concept of 'face', which is a sort of combination of honour, respect and good reputation. You must avoid losing face or *causing* loss of face at all times.

From a Chinese point of view that means, for instance, staying silent if you disagree with somebody, especially if that person is senior to you. Rank is regarded as very important and you must treat people with due deference or you'll lose their business. For the same reason, you should arrive on time for meetings or slightly early.

Lengthy eye contact may be considered disrespectful, which can make initial greetings seem slightly uncomfortable when the person gently shaking your hand is staring fixedly at the floor. They're being polite. Always greet people in order of seniority. Hand them your business card, which should have been translated on one side into simple Chinese characters printed in the auspicious colour gold.

Meetings are often arranged through an intermediary who can vouch for you and your company. Documentation translated into Chinese should have been sent in advance. If you are using visual materials, restrict them to black type on a white background as colours may be interpreted as inauspicious.

Remember the Chinese have a very strong group identity and they'll also see you as a representative of your company. In negotiations, only senior representatives will speak. Make sure you designate your speaker too. In the end, they'll never say no outright; they're protecting *your* face. But maybe they'll say yes.

JOBS AND VISAS

With rapid economic growth creating a substantial skills shortage, it's easy for just about anybody with qualifications, expertise and a little experience to get a good job in China. Well, it is as long as you speak fluent Mandarin.

That is a slight exaggeration. Language skills do remain extremely important, but with the increasing number of foreign companies establishing a base in China, it is possible to get a job without speaking much Mandarin or Cantonese if you have the right skills. 'Multinationals in Greater China are committed to an increasingly local business approach. Chinese language skills have become a prerequisite for most management positions that require staff to deal with local clients, partners, vendors, distributors and colleagues. Of all the job listings we have ever been involved in recruiting for, over 95 per cent required the candidate to speak Mandarin at a fairly fluent level,' explains Lawrence C Wang, managing director and founder of recruitment agency Wang & Li Asia Resources.

The largest group of English-speaking workers in China are language teachers, and there's no shortage of jobs. Pay is good (by local standards) for a single person. Bringing children, however, would probably be prohibitively expensive because of the high fees for their education. That cost, however, reveals another opportunity. The growth of international schools teaching in English has been phenomenal. They are serving not just the expat community, but are also the places where the burgeoning Chinese middle class aspires to send its children. Qualified British teachers are in demand, so subsidised fees may be part of the package that would make it possible to turn this posting into one for all the family. It is still probably easier if you aren't married.

The downside as far as the huge demand for teachers is concerned is that it has attracted unscrupulous employers. Usually their prey are backpackers working their way round Asia who'll take the risk of working illegally. Fortunately, it's not that easy to break the law accidentally. The procedure, if you're offered a job in China, is that you are given a 'Z' visa, which is valid for 30 days. During that period, the holder must go through the residential formalities at the local public security department and their hiring company must process their Alien Working Permit or Foreign Expert's Licence.

'F' visas are given to foreigners who wish to participate in a business conference, short-term course, on-the-job training, or scientific-technological and cultural exchanges for a period not longer than six months. 'L' visas are given to tourists. You cannot work on an 'F' or an 'L' visa.

The job market for foreigners in China has changed as the economy has grown. 'Companies don't usually expatriate people to China these days unless the person is at a fairly senior management level and already has a proven track record in the company,' says Wang. That means it's less easy to find jobs which combine a Western level of pay with a Chinese cost of living. Skilled professionals may find work which is well paid by Chinese standards, but will not leave much over for contributions to your pension fund.

With so many companies and such a fast-growing economy, there are a huge number of ways into the job market. It is worth approaching head hunters or 'executive search' agencies and making sure they have your curriculum vitae. There are also large numbers of online English-language recruitment sites, as a quick Internet search will reveal. These tend to focus largely on teaching jobs. The Hong Kong-based *South China Morning Post* (www.scmp.com) newspaper also has mainland jobs. Professionals are recruited through advertisements in international specialist and business publications too. Alternatively, you could try approaching companies directly. Wang suggests getting hold of the directories of companies published by the Chambers of Commerce and industry associations in Shanghai and Beijing. He also says it's worth addressing your request to the general manager or country manager rather than the human resources department.

STARTING YOUR OWN BUSINESS IN CHINA

As with finding a job, starting a business is a lot easier if you can speak fluent Mandarin. Equally, the visa system tends to be geared to people coming to do a specific job. So the popular strategy for the growing number of foreigners starting a business in China is to take a post – teaching English, say – and combine this with carrying out research into potential business opportunities and polishing up their Chinese language skills.

The process of starting a business in China has become easier. It is, for instance, no longer a legal requirement for foreigners to set up a joint venture with a local partner. There may be times when it is expedient to work with somebody who knows and understands the local market, but it is no longer compulsory. The Chinese government has less fear of foreigners taking over their businesses.

The trepidation may have gone away, but not the Chinese attitude to foreigners. For centuries and explicitly through Mao, the belief has been that foreign things should serve China. It's an uncomfortably pragmatic attitude that has left no shortage of bitter individuals who believe they were treated unfairly or pushed out of successful businesses.

Knowing the attitude that underlies dealings with foreigners should help you tailor your business plans accordingly. Look to see how you can be seen to be aiding the development of the economy. That's not just manufacturing, but the provision of 'soft' skills such as language education, management and the development of creative talent.

Many of the requirements are stated explicitly in five-year plans. These list, for instance, whether foreign investment projects are prohibited, restricted or encouraged. It's a valuable guide.

The downside of the direct political involvement of the Chinese Communist Party is that policies can change quite suddenly. Also, in common with other countries with a powerful bureaucracy, there's a tendency to turn a blind eye to certain practices which may not be licensed or legal. Then there'll be a sudden clampdown.

Often these practices developed because of the difficulty in keeping up with the rapid changes in regulations and licensing requirements. This is where it becomes vitally important to get the right advice and support. You'll almost certainly need to get involved in the expat networks for this. China is not the sort of country where you are able to blend in with the locals.

You can also take advantage of some of the online expat forums which can be an invaluable source of information that you can't find elsewhere, especially in English. Try www.chinaexpat.com, www.expatsinchina.com or www.thechinaexpat.com. For general business advice, the best starting point I've found is the China-Britain Business Council. Its website is: www.cbbc.org.

Finally, the best way of keeping track of what's happening in the Middle Kingdom is through the Danwei blog (www.danwei.org). It's edited by

Jeremy Goldkorn who is a living example of how it's possible to be foreign and successful in business in China. A South African, he moved to China in 1995, cycled across Xinjiang and Tibet, and has spent the last decade working in the Chinese media, advertising and Internet industries.

BUYING PROPERTY IN CHINA

There are huge variations in the price and standard of property to rent across this vast country. The chances are, however, that expats will be looking for a place to stay in one of the big cities.

It's safest to use an agency although with little regulation it's not always easy to find a good one. Ask around. Use the expat online bulletin boards. And if you're not sure about a particular company, walk away. There are so many that there'll be another one round the corner. And all of them are getting a substantial commission of which you'll be expected to pay half.

Many of the agencies are local. The easiest way to find them is with a quick online search. Of course this won't find every agency, but it will locate those that are most likely to be able to understand expat requirements.

Prices aren't cheap, but much of the accommodation to rent especially in cities is of a high standard and comes fully furnished, often with an ADSL line. As in any country, you should check the inventory carefully and counter-sign it with the landlord. Beware of the friendly landlord, by the way, who offers you a contract only in Chinese. Expats have ended up agreeing to extortionate rent rises. Make sure you have a translated version of any document you sign, although it's the Chinese version that will be recognised in court.

Most leases are for a year, although it is possible to find places for six months. The landlord will ask for a deposit of between one and three months' rent which should be refunded once you've returned the property in good condition. The landlord should also register you with the local police within a month. Ensure this task has been carried out or you could face a hefty fine.

For longer stays, purchasing a property *is* an option, but be prepared for more than a few sleepless nights if you do decide to buy. Nothing stays the same or is quite what it seems. The market combines being relatively unregulated with a large amount of government interference. So, for instance, in 2006 the government announced that more than 60 per cent of the land deals in the previous two years were illegal because there had not been central approval. It was often local officials who had made the sales. At the same time, there is little legal protection for buyers.

Logically, the lack of regulation combined with China's rapid economic growth should create a boom in property prices. That's where the state interference comes in. Worried about a speculative housing bubble, the government keeps introducing measures to make purchase difficult. The amount of deposit required was raised to 50 per cent, minimum mortgage rates have been increased and capital gains tax of 20 per cent is payable on properties sold within two years of purchase.

The measures have been successful so far at keeping the price of property far more affordable in cities such as Shanghai and Beijing than in Tokyo or Hong Kong. The relatively low prices can make property attractive to expats, especially as there's a feeling that the government may not be able to keep the lid on prices for ever.

For anybody thinking of taking the plunge, the lack of transparency and clear rules makes finding the right experienced people absolutely vital. They won't just protect your purchase, but they can also help negotiate the best price–especially when government measures to stop an unsustainable boom have created a buyer's market.

There are definite pitfalls to be avoided. Buying off-plan is popular in many countries and can save you money in China, but the lack of consumer protection makes it risky. There are endless horror stories of people arriving in their new homes to find crumbling walls, ill-fitting windows and leaking roofs with nobody to turn to for recompense.

Research is vital. You'll almost certainly be buying a new property as there's not much of a resale market. Look at other work from the developer and see if the quality is up to scratch. Ask the residents if you can. Also find out which property management company is in charge of the development. A good one can smooth out many problems. Finally check to see that local amenities have kept up with the pace of construction.

HONG KONG

At the start of the lengthy negotiations that eventually led to Britain's handover of Hong Kong to China, there was stark difference between the two economic systems. The British colony represented the ultimate in unfettered capitalism, while China was rigidly communist.

From the British side, the principal concern was that Hong Kong's economic freedoms should continue. Britain also argued that there should be democracy (but given that it had never got round to introducing democracy in the colony, this was a rather harder point to argue). While the negotiations were going on, China was changing. The Communist Party was still very much in charge, but it was introducing reforms which it justified ideologically through some rather convoluted logic as being 'socialist', but to everybody else looked like capitalism.

Since the handover, China has fulfilled two roles in Hong Kong. It has remained a powerful financial centre. But increasingly it has become a stepping stone into the booming Chinese economy. More than 20 per cent of China's foreign trade passes through Hong Kong.

QUICK FACTS

- **Land area:** 1,098 square kilometres
- **Population:** 6.9 million
- **Climate:** Hong Kong's summers tend to be hot and humid with occasional thunderstorms and tropical cyclones. The winters, particularly November and December, are generally more pleasant.
- **Main languages:** Chinese (mainly Cantonese), English (an 'official language' and first language of about three per cent of the population)
- **Currency:** Hong Kong dollar (£1 = HK$15.27, January 2008)
- **How long does it take to get there from the UK?** Flights from London to Hong Kong take approximately 12 hours.
- **How many British migrants are there?** There are no separate figures for Hong Kong since the handover. However, it is believed that the numbers have dropped by up to 90 per cent, leaving just a few thousand British expats.

- **Cost of living:** Hong Kong has consistently been one of the most expensive places in the world to live. The main factor is the shortage of land – and therefore property – which pushes the price of accommodation to astronomical levels. The flip side of this is that it's a very compact place to live, with cheap and plentiful public transport. Ideally, you'll find an employer who will provide accommodation and, preferably, health cover as well. The other item which is expensive is education.

THE HONG KONG ECONOMY

The 1997 handover coincided with the regional Asian economic crisis and the inevitable uncertainty that accompanies a change in political power. Within a couple of years, however, the economy had begun to bounce back only to be hit again in 2000 when the dot-com bubble burst.

Another cautious recovery was almost derailed by the 9/11 events in the United States and again by the SARS outbreak in 2003. Hong Kong's economy, however, has always been highly cyclical and generally the signs are that it has been relatively unaffected by the handover. Property prices, for instance, are regarded as a robust indicator of economic health and they're higher than ever. In the longer term, though, the geographically better placed city of Shanghai with its proximity to Japan and greater room for expansion could displace Hong Kong as the financial centre of the region.

DOING BUSINESS IN HONG KONG

Generally the etiquette differs little from the mainland. The long period of British rule does, however, mean that local people are rather more accustomed to dealing with westerners. It would, however, be a mistake to come on like an old colonial.

In some areas, particularly in the financial sector, attitudes and behaviour may differ little from Europe and North America. Elsewhere business relationships are more traditional. You'll just have to play it by ear.

JOBS AND VISAS

It used to be very easy for British passport holders to get work in Hong Kong. English is one of the two official languages, along with Cantonese, and many of the companies retained strong British links.

Some estimates put the fall in the number of Brits in the former colony as high as 90 per cent since the handover of sovereignty. There is still, however, a very close-knit English-speaking expat community. It's the one part of China where it's still possible to find work without speaking the local language, although this is becoming harder and harder.

The ideal way of working in Hong Kong is to be posted there by a multinational company. That should at least get you over the biggest hurdle, which is the exorbitant price of property to rent in the former colony. This route is becoming increasingly less common as multinational companies find it much cheaper to hire locals.

You can also apply for jobs directly in Hong Kong and there's no shortage of online resources. For a start have a look at: www.hongkong.recruit.net, www.newchinacareer.com or the local version of Monster, www.monster.com.hk. Advertising and applying for jobs through websites is well established, so looking for work this way is more effective than in many other countries.

You can try to find a job after you've arrived on a tourist visa. It's not easy, but it's not impossible either. The advantage is that you'll be available immediately for interview and can network more effectively. On the other hand the authorities don't want to encourage people to come looking for work.

Whichever way you find employment you'll need the appropriate the visa and work permit. Details are subject to change, but you'll generally find the most up-to date information on the Hong Kong Immigration Department's website: www.immd.gov.hk. The key areas that the authorities will look at before providing the permit are: whether a post could be filled by an existing resident; the established status of the company offering a job and your qualifications to fill the post.

Hong Kong is an increasingly service-based economy, with manufacturing having moved to the nearby Chinese mainland. The financial sector offers the best job prospects for foreigners, along with support services such as IT.

BUYING AND RENTING PROPERTY

Although rents are never low in Hong Kong, there are fairly wide disparities according to where you choose to live. Broadly speaking, the further away you live from the central business district the cheaper it gets. But before you grab an apparent bargain, do spend some time in the neighbourhood to make sure you can cope with the commuting and distance from the famous nightlife. Mistakes can be expensive.

Tenancy agreements in Hong Kong are usually for two years with penalties if you leave early. Landlords expect two to three months' rent as a deposit, which is refunded at the end of the lease minus the costs of repairs and replacements for anything not considered fair wear and tear. An agency will also take half-a-month's rent as commission.

Apartments in Hong Kong are generally leased unfurnished, although many do have appliances including washing machines, refrigerators and air-conditioning already fitted. Rents don't usually cover management fees or government taxes which together add another 12–15 per cent to your outgoings. Tenants are also responsible for utility connection and payments.

The bottom line is that before you take on a tenancy, you'll need to have sufficient funds to pay: four-and-a-half months rent to the landlord and agent; deposits to the utility companies and enough to cover the cost of furnishings. The traditional place to look for property is in the *South China Morning Post* on a Wednesday. Alternatively, a quick online search will reveal a long list of agencies with properties for sale or rent.

There's no restriction buying property, apart from the exorbitant cost. The process remains similar to the English system. Estate agents are licensed. Normally the buyer will put down an initial deposit of five per cent, then another five per cent a fortnight later when the formal agreement is signed. Completion and full payment takes place after six to eight weeks.

Finding the right place is time-consuming and there are one or two quirks. Property on any floor with a four in it is a little cheaper because the Cantonese words for 'four' and 'death' sound similar. A view of a cemetery can also knock money off the price.

JAPAN

There are few countries in Asia where it's relatively easy for an English speaker to get work. In fact, it's hard to think of any other with an advanced economy. Japan, however, remains fascinatingly exotic.

And that's a feeling that cuts two ways. Many Westerners who've lived in Japan for a while enjoy a sort of celebrity status. In many places, foreigners remain a rarity. Most expats stay only for a few months, but for a few it's a move that lasts a lifetime.

Quick facts

- **Land area:** 380,000 square kilometres
- **Population:** 127.7 million
- **Climate:** Japan's seasons are very distinct. Spring is pleasant with low rainfall and cherry blossom. Summer starts wet in June then turns hot and humid. September sees the start of autumn which is comfortable, and accompanied by spectacular colours as the leaves turn. Winter's the ski season and wouldn't be too bad if central heating was more common.
- **Language:** Japanese
- **Currency:** The Yen (£1 = 214 yen, January 2008)
- **How long does it take to get there?** A flight from London to Tokyo takes 12 hours
- **How many British migrants are there?** At the time of writing, there are 23,000 British people in Japan.
- **Cost of living:** Tokyo is famous for being one of the world's most expensive cities and it is certainly is if you live in the centre of the city and enjoy the high life. Live more like the Japanese in the suburbs, however, and it's not so horrendous. Running a car is expensive, as are utilities. Stick to seasonal Japanese food from supermarkets rather than buying imported products and you'll keep your shopping bill down. Also, if you're Western-sized, buy your clothes when you're back in the UK.

THE ECONOMY

For a long time the Japanese economy boomed, thanks partly to the way manufacturers, suppliers, and distributors worked closely-knit groups called 'keiretsu'. It also benefited from having very little military expenditure since the end of the Second World War

The late 1980s became known as 'the bubble'. It burst in 1990: the stock market tumbled and there followed a decade of stagnation. The economy has, however, been growing strongly since 2003. It remains the second largest in the world, but there remain underlying problems. It's inflexible (by modern standards) in that Japanese men tend to have the same employer throughout their working lives. The population is also ageing fast.

The government has been trying – with limited success – to encourage increased inward investment from overseas companies, partly because it is hoped that the foreign competition will inspire local companies.

DOING BUSINESS IN JAPAN

All the stories you've heard about the formality of Japanese business culture probably have some basis in truth. Fortunately the Japanese are also very polite so any early faux pas that you commit may just help to break the ice.

You should dress very soberly: dark suit in winter, grey suit in summer. Don't wear a loud tie, but don't go too far the other way: black is regarded as funereal. Women should also dress for a formal office setting, but be aware that female executives are still something of a rarity.

When you meet somebody for the first time, don't grab them by the hand and start shaking it. The Japanese can be quite uncomfortable with demonstrative physical contact of any sort. Also remember that business cards have great symbolic importance. Make sure you have plenty. Have them printed in English on one side with a Japanese translation on the other. Present the card with both hands to the most senior person at a meeting. Accept a proffered card with both hands, say thank you and bow slightly. Never fiddle with business cards or make notes on them. And make sure you collect all the cards you've been given at the end of a meeting.

When you arrive at a meeting, try to get there a few minutes before the scheduled start-time. Once the meeting begins, wait to be seated: there's an ancient etiquette to that too. Take plenty of notes – it shows you're interested – and expect the meeting to finish exactly on time. Japanese business schedules tend to be tight.

ACCOMMODATION

Renting property in Japan is extremely expensive, and not just because of the rent: you also have to pay up front for deposits and commissions. These charges can easily equal six months' rent and they're not always returnable. And this assumes you'll find a company that will let to foreigners, which is far from easy.

As a result, many people new to the country start off by living in what are known as guest houses or *gaijin* houses. The majority of these are in Tokyo, but they can also be found in other major cities. Most of the *gaijin* houses are apartments in slightly run-down blocks. Some are private apartments, others have a shared bathroom or kitchen. Generally, you get what you pay for. Furnishing is usually fairly basic, but will probably include some cooking utensils, a futon and a pay phone.

WORK

The most common job for English speakers is teaching: there's an almost insatiable demand from large and small private schools, secondary schools and for private tutors. Turnover is high, although rates of pay aren't bad for somebody who is young, free and single. Older would-be expats should probably look elsewhere.

Many jobs are advertised online. The website for *The Japan Times* (www.japantimes.co.jp) has a good selection, as does www.jobsinjapan.com. Ideally, you'd apply with your CV and be offered a job. The language school would them sponsor you so you could get a legitimate work visa. Unfortunately, it doesn't usually work like that, and most appointments take place after a face-to-face interview. What you should probably do, therefore, is travel to Japan on a tourist visa and set up meetings once you get there. There's nothing illegal about doing this, although it's not necessarily a good idea to declare to the immigration authorities that the purpose of your visit is anything other than tourism.

Once you've got a job and a sponsor, you shouldn't really start working until you have the correct visa. In fact, many people ignore this law, mainly because the authorities are said to be more concerned about over-stayers than people working on tourist visas. A better alternative is to leave the country and re-enter a short time later with the correct visa.

Although teaching is the main occupation for foreigners, especially when they've just arrived, it's not the only option. Many companies use native English speakers to rewrite documents for international markets. Your Western looks may get you a job as a model or an actor. As ever, the best way to work is often through a posting from a multinational company – a good number of them, particularly in the financial sector, have a presence in Japan. Most recruit senior staff in their home country then hire local Japanese workers. Sometimes, however, if they are approached directly they may hire expats. It's probably a matter of luck.

Pay in Japan, even for teachers, isn't bad and tax rates are very low. Some jobs also offer quite an attractive package of extras including subsidised accommodation and so on.

STARTING A BUSINESS

Japan would certainly be one of the last stable, advanced capitalist economies where I'd try to start a business. But it seems there's nowhere in the world that doesn't have some British entrepreneur toiling away.

Neil Riley quit his secure job with Deutsche Bank in Japan to set up the specialist skiing company Welovesnow.com. 'I think I chose to set up a company in the most heavily regulated industry within the most heavily regulated capitalist market in the world,' he told me.

Even with local partners and his industry background, opening an account with one of the notoriously risk-averse Japanese banks was difficult. Then he became the first foreigner to apply for a travel agent's licence. 'That meant I had to be recommended by two other travel agents. That's an interesting reflection on Japanese culture because you're essentially approaching two competitors.'

Riley is happy to admit that now he is through the maze of regulation, there are advantages, not least the same barriers that other potential entrants to the market face. But, challenging though setting up his company has been, the type of business is not unlike many others across the globe. The tourist product might be Japanese, but his customers are overwhelmingly English speaking.

How about selling to the Japanese? It can be done. Brian Tannura's business story starts at the end of the 1990s when he was teaching English at a large Japanese language school. 'It wasn't so much that I wanted to be my own boss, but I knew I didn't want to have a boss,' he says.

As was the fashion, he tried various Internet ventures, none of which provided sufficient income for him to quit his job. Then, back home in the US, he saw a giant, talking gumball machine. To say that the Japanese are nuts about vending machines is an understatement. There's estimated to be one machine for every 23 people in the country. For Tannura, the maths also made sense. The largest standard coin in the US is a quarter - worth about 13 pence at the time of writing. In Japan, most vending machines take 100 yen coins, currently worth around 43p.

So he bought the gumball machine using his credit card and had it shipped to Japan. It didn't work. The local Osaka power supply runs at 60 hertz and his machine needed 50 hertz. Unabashed, he used his plastic to buy and import three 60 hertz machines. He managed to get these placed at prime locations at an amusement park and a large department store - in return for providing room for a machine the site owner receives a healthy slice of the profit. Tannura is responsible for stocking, repairing and emptying out the coins.

As the gumball business grew, he had a chance meeting with a businessman who had a number of machines for selling stickers, a concept that had never caught on in Japan. Tannura thought this might be because the local material was fairly dull and generic. In the US and Canada, kids had been buying sets of stickers for 20 or 30 years, so he started to import those. And they caught on. He's now adding two or three machines a day to his empire.

His way of working is as far removed as it's possible to be from the Internet models he flirted with. 'I count the coins and know within a week whether a machine in a particular location is working,' he says. Growth has been funded entirely without borrowing apart from the initial credit card payments.

Asked whether it was more or less difficult to start a business in Japan, Tannura doesn't know. 'I've never launched a business anywhere else,' he says. But he does recognise some advantages, not least the willingness of Japanese banks to let customers pay in large bags of unsorted coins. 'They might not like it, but it is part of the service.'

If there's a lesson in this, it's probably that if the person and the product are right, language and nationality don't really matter. Tannura now plans to turn his company, Market Pioneer Japan, into a global player.

MIDDLE EAST

SAUDI ARABIA

Since the 1970s, the attraction of Saudi Arabia for foreign workers has been simple. Money. Okay, living in the kingdom might be fascinating, but it seems unlikely that many non-Muslims would choose to spend years in a strict Islamic state without substantial financial inducements.

Actually, these days the salaries don't look astronomical in comparison with those in many Western countries. What makes the difference is the lack of income tax and the payment of a substantial bonus at the end of a contract. At the same time, workers can save a large proportion of their income because remuneration packages generally include accommodation and other living expenses; annual flights to home countries and other benefits.

QUICK FACTS

- **Land area:** 2.24 million square kilometres
- **Population:** 25.6 million
- **Climate:** Although Saudi is one of the driest countries in the world, that only tells part of the story. On the Red Sea and the Persian Gulf, humidity is often unpleasantly high, even though maximum temperatures are lower than inland. Away from the coast, the desert climate often means very high daytime temperatures with an abrupt drop at night. Either way, it's a land of air conditioning.
- **Main language:** Arabic
- **Currency:** Riyal (£1 = 7.4 riyals August 2007)
- **How long does it take to get there from the UK and are flights all the year round?** Direct flights from London take between six and seven hours. Frequencies are the same at all times of year.
- **How many British migrants are there?** 26,000
- **Cost of living:** Goods which are normally taxed elsewhere are markedly cheaper in tax-free Saudi, but imported foods may be expensive. Utilities

are generally fairly cheap, although it's not hard to run up a substantial electricity bill using air conditioning. Accommodation is going to be the largest single monthly outgoing you'll probably face. A prospective employer should be able to tell you how much an unfurnished apartment will cost in the appropriate foreigners' compound.

THE ECONOMY

As the world's biggest oil exporter, there are no prizes for guessing what drives the Saudi economy. This created absolutely phenomenal growth during the boom years of the 1970s and a precipitate decline in the 1980s. Since that boom and bust, the government has taken steps to reduce the country's reliance on a single commodity, no matter how valuable it might be. Money has been spent on infrastructure, training and development, with some success.

The challenge has often been to continue developing non-oil interests when the worldwide increase in the price of oil has meant income continues to pour into the kingdom.

DOING BUSINESS IN SAUDI ARABIA

The key point to realise is that Saudi Arabia is not egalitarian. It's not just women who are treated differently, either: as a foreigner of either sex you will not be regarded as an equal. That is not to say the Saudis are anything less than extremely hospitable, but you will be kept waiting when you arrive for a meeting (assuming it's not cancelled at the last minute).

Once in the meeting, there'll be prolonged small talk. The only real taboo is that you should not enquire after your host's wife, as this may be regarded as disrespectful. When you do finally get onto business, there's a fair chance you'll be interrupted.

Negotiations are slow, starting from a very high or very low point. Be careful not to get over-excited when you seem to have made a breakthrough. Saudis feel it is rude to say no and can seem to over-compensate by saying 'yes' in an over-exuberant way when what is meant is 'maybe'. Be patient.

JOBS AND VISAS

In recent years, the government has tried to reduce the dependence on foreign workers by training more Saudis. It will take time for this to have a profound effect and in the short term has increased the demand for training professionals. In addition, there is a continuing need for health professionals, teachers, IT specialists, financial experts, defence workers and other professionals. And, of course, the oil industry continues to provide work for large numbers of foreign nationals.

These days, there are few Westerners involved in semi-skilled jobs. Partly that's because the massive construction projects where they were employed have now been completed, but more importantly, this type of labour is recruited almost exclusively from developing countries such as Pakistan, Bangladesh and the Philippines. These countries also provide most of the unskilled service workers.

Most recruitment is through agencies in workers' home countries. These tend to specialise in professional areas rather than being geographically specific, so medical agencies will deal with doctors and nurses, and so on. Executive positions are often filled using head-hunters. In each case it's the employer who pays the commission.

Contracts used to be for fixed periods of two or three years, although they could be renewed, but they are now sometimes open ended. You'll still need a work visa, which normally needs to be renewed every three years. To request one, you'll need to apply via the Saudi embassy in London: the consular services section of the Ministry of Foreign Affairs' website (www.mofa.gov.sa – click the 'English' tab at the top) explains the process and the documents you'll need to supply, which include:

- relevant application form
- current passport with at least six months left to run
- medical report (your doctor can conduct a medical, which will include a mandatory test for HIV/AIDS

WHAT'S IT LIKE TO WORK IN SAUDI?

Very few people who come to Saudi Arabia to work avoid the experience of profound culture shock. They come knowing the country is the centre of the Islamic religion with two of its most holy shrines, Mecca and Medina, and it is governed with strict adherence to *sharia* law. It is not a democracy, but an absolute monarchy.

One of the less well-known proscriptions is that photography is banned. That may go some way to explaining why the day-to-day impact of the religious laws hasn't been well-documented for Western eyes.

Sarah and Marcele (not their real names) actually met in Saudi when she was working as a flight attendant for an airline and he was executive chef at a hotel in Jeddah. 'Courting was very different to how we know it in Europe. I was never really able to relax and had the feeling of always being watched. I felt as though I was a cheat and "dirty",' Sarah says.

Many expats have these sort of feelings, which stem from the unusual lifestyle. Most live on compounds where there are some Western freedoms, but no alcohol. Outside, Westerners are subject to the same restrictions as Saudis. Largely that means sexes are not allowed to mix and women must cover all flesh and hair. Infringements are punished by the religious police.

Sarah says that expats often feel that they've had their identity stolen. 'The paradox is that one is largely dependent on the Saudi entourage for most material requirements. This requires staying "on good terms" with the people one is dependent on and takes away any personal choices or independence. You therefore feel vulnerable and oppressed. Strong feelings of "them and me" are encountered, along with loneliness, isolation and even bitterness towards the Saudis.

'As a woman, these feelings are usually stronger as you have to accept that you will never be independent. Saudis treat women as second class citizens,' she continues. Eventually she started counselling to regain a loss of self-confidence.

It's not just women who can feel a loss of independence. Marcele explains: 'On arrival, I wasn't allowed to drive on my French licence. I had to be sponsored by a Saudi citizen from my company who would present me for the Saudi driving test. If I passed this I would be allowed to buy a car and drive.'

When he arrived in Saudi, there was no car insurance because of the belief that only Allah could decide what happens to you. Despite misgivings in some quarters, compulsory motor insurance has now been introduced which is perhaps just as well given the large number of expensive vehicles and the high accident rate in the Kingdom.

Marcele also faced other problems, including language issues, thanks to the Saudi practice of recruiting different groups of workers from different countries. 'The kitchen staff were all of Asian origin and hardly spoke any English (let alone French!). My task was to put the hotel kitchen back on its feet within a tight time frame, which proved very difficult when dealing with staff with whom I could not communicate,' he said.

Sarah and Marcele are now married and living in France running a bed-and-breakfast business. They wouldn't go back to Saudi to work, but both are intrigued to see what happens to the place which brought them together and helped to finance their new life.

UNITED ARAB EMIRATES (UAE)

There are actually seven emirates: Dubai, Abu Dhabi, Ajman, Fujairah, Ras al-Khaimah, Sharjah and Umm al-Quwain, but it's the first two, with their phenomenally fast-growing economies, that most westerners have heard of. They've always been seen as places of high pay, no tax and more freedom than Saudi.

In the last decade, Dubai has transformed itself into a desirable destination with amazing hotels, restaurants and everything else that goes to make up a world-class tourist resort, apart possibly from any sense of history. It has certainly become a place where people want to work rather than simply going to earn money. But now you need the money to enjoy the lifestyle.

QUICK FACTS

- **Land area:** 83,600 square kilometres
- **Population:** 2.5 million
- **Language:** Arabic
- **Climate:** Although there's little rainfall, summers can be extremely humid with temperatures reaching 50 degrees Celsius. (That's not a misprint.) Winter, from October to March, on the other hand is pleasantly dry and warm, although night-time temperatures can be slightly chilly.
- **Currency:** Dirham (£1 = 7.4 dirham, January 2008)
- **How long does it take to get there from the UK and are services year round?** Flying from London to Dubai takes roughly seven hours. There are flights all year.
- **How many British migrants are there?** 55,000
- **Cost of living:** It's often not so much that Dubai is expensive, but that there are so many things to spend money on. From world-class shopping to great restaurants, sports clubs and stunning beaches, it can feel like paradise. But it all comes at a price. Having made the place so attractive, employers don't need to offer so many perks, so free medical allowances and private schooling have disappeared from contracts. And education in particular is extremely expensive. The price of property to rent or buy is also spiralling ever upwards.

THE ECONOMY

However you measure it, the UAE has one of the fastest growing economies in the world. Oil has been the foundation, but the government has successfully moved the focus away from the total reliance on oil.

Dubai's achievements in construction are best known, with perhaps the most revealing statistic being the presence in 2006 of 30,000 of the world's mobile cranes, just under of a quarter of the world's total. Otherwise it's a list of superlatives, including: the world's tallest tower; largest shopping mall; most expensive hotel and the biggest Guggenheim Museum.

Although the buildings are most conspicuous, in terms of employment it's the economic 'Freezones' that are the most important development.

These are free of taxes and the restrictions on ownership that exist elsewhere.

Dubai Internet City has attracted IT giants including: Microsoft, Oracle, HP, IBM, Compaq, Dell, Siemens, Canon, Logica, Sony Ericsson and Cisco and a community of thousands of knowledge workers. The Media City is designed to attract businesses such as broadcasting, publishing, advertising, public relations, research, music and post-production. Jabel Ali Freezone aspires to be the international business hub of the Middle East. The Airport Freezone, meanwhile, focuses on the production of low volume, high value goods which are suitable for air transport.

Generally these Freezones are seen as being a major achievement. There are, however, a few storm clouds on the horizon. Success breeds imitators and there are now other Middle Eastern countries, such as Egypt and Jordan, competing for some of the same business. The other price of such rapid growth is the threat of inflation. In the longer term, Abu Dhabi's slower development might be more effective.

Finally, with any Islamic country there is the threat of fundamentalism. So far the UAE has managed to walk a tightrope, with the government continuing its commitment to preserving the traditional culture. Almost half the guest workers, however, are Hindu, Christian or Buddhist. More potentially problematic is the Internet City, which is theoretically subject to the same censorship as the rest of the country.

DOING BUSINESS IN THE UAE

Although this may be one of the most liberal parts of the Middle East, it is still a Muslim country. Act accordingly. Your hosts may be so polite that you may not know you've offended them until your dealings dry up.

Dress conservatively and women should take care not to reveal flesh. Address people as *Sayed* (Mr) or *Sayeda* (Mrs) followed by their first name.

Many meetings take place over lunch and this may be far more formal than in the west. Greet them effusively when you meet them, shaking hands then touching your heart with your right hand to show sincerity. Be prepared for small talk to go on for a long time before the real reason for the meeting comes up. That can happen quite suddenly and be resolved equally quickly.

Whatever you do, don't order alcohol with your meal as this may deeply offend your Muslim contacts. Equally, if you're eating in traditional style sitting on the floor, ensure the soles of your feet do not point at anybody even accidentally.

The final point to remember is that bargaining is part of the culture. A seller will start with a price probably twice as high as is hoped for and the buyer will begin from a correspondingly low position. It may take some time to reach the middle ground.

JOBS AND VISAS

Most foreigners find work in the Emirates in a similar way to jobs in Saudi, that is through agencies in their home countries. These tend to specialise in specific areas of recruitment such as medical, IT or education.

Westerners are generally hired for skilled jobs while the majority of labourers come from countries such as Bangladesh, Pakistan and India. If you suspect there may be some implicit racism involved, you wouldn't be wrong. People from these poorer countries often work excessively long hours in extreme temperatures for low pay. The government is making some effort to improve their position, but there's a long way to go.

The position for Westerners is better, but do check any contract very carefully. Tax-free salaries can look most attractive, but accommodation prices, in particular, are horrendous and landlords expect the whole year's rent up front. Make sure your pay really is as good as it looks.

Once you've been offered a job you'll have to apply for an employment visa. You have to use this within two months of it being issued. It is then valid for 30 days during which time your sponsoring company has to complete the rest of the formalities.

STARTING A BUSINESS

It is also possible to start your own business or be self-employed in the UAE. In both cases, it's something that can only really be achieved when you're already living and working in the region. It's not something you can do on your own without the close involvement of locals. To become self-employed you need a sponsor, either an individual citizen or a company. They will be paid either a flat fee or a percentage of your revenue. Either way, be prepared for some tough bargaining and get a good lawyer.

Starting a business also requires local involvement, this time in the form of a partner who will take a majority stake in the company (although that doesn't mean he has to put any money in). The Ministry of Commerce (www.commerce.gov.sa/english) will also expect proof that you have a considerable amount of money to invest. Once again, a good lawyer is vital to ensure you get over all the bureaucratic hurdles.

Despite the risks and hassles, the economy is growing so fast that there are some excellent opportunities for entrepreneurs. The government can also be very supportive. It is, after all, trying to turn the area into a sort of new Hong Kong of the Middle East.

PROPERTY AND ACCOMMODATION

Despite the huge amount of property being built, the price of rental accommodation has continued to rise. There is a cap on increases which is set every year in Dubai, but it has been consistently above the rate of inflation.

Most rentals are through estate agents and there are plenty of listings online including the *Gulf News* site (www.gnads4u.com) and the *Khaleej Times* (www.khaleejtimes.com). You can haggle over prices.

Once you find a place, you'll probably have to pay the whole year's rent in advance. Some landlords will allow you to do this with up to four post-dated cheques. An agency will require a five per cent commission. There will also be a security deposit and a deposit for utilities which are the responsibility of the tenant. There may also be a municipal tax on top.

Until relatively recently expats couldn't buy freehold property in the UAE, despite their desire to stop paying huge sums to landlords with nothing to show for it at the end of the year. Even now purchases are restricted to designated areas. Ownership does not guarantee a permanent residence visa or the right to work in Dubai.

The legal uncertainty that existed around ownership also meant it was difficult to get mortgages on property. Now banks such as Barclays are offering up to 90 per cent of the purchase price. It's an attractive alternative to renting for anybody planning to spend some time in the UAE.

Anybody deciding to buy should try to have their finances in place in advance of making a decision. The purchase process can be surprisingly swift so it's better to have a pre-approved mortgage.

Given the pace of development, most foreigners end up buying off-plan before the property has been built. It is obviously worth looking, if possible, at other places the construction company has completed to get a better idea of what your future home will look like when it's completed.

Generally, you pay a fairly small deposit then 10 to 20 per cent of the price of the property every three months. This does mean you're paying the developer's costs, however, the UAE laws do seem to have prevented the problems which have existed in other countries where companies have gone bust taking purchasers' money with them.

WHAT'S IT LIKE TO LIVE AND WORK IN DUBAI?

Keith Williamson ended up in the Middle East in 1993 when he escaped from recession in the construction industry in the UK. 'A former colleague had worked for many years in Kuwait, and through one of his contacts in the region he told me about a position in Riyadh. It was a one-year contract, bachelor status, and the salary looked like it would keep the wolf from the door. So I took it and had a totally horrible year in Saudi Arabia,' he says.

'While I was there I heard good things about this little place called Dubai, so I decided to stop over there for a few days at the end of my contract. As luck would have it, another former colleague was setting up a design business and he offered me a job there and then.'

Keith then went back to the UK, packed up his stuff, and a few months later he was living with his wife and his then primary school-aged son in Dubai. To begin with, he worked as an interior designer before moving into freelance Web design seven years ago.

The changes that have brought highly-paid work haven't always been good to live with. 'Dubai has been one massive construction site for about the last five years. The construction has brought massive congestion with it, so the large town that we used to live in, where you could drive anywhere in about ten minutes, is now a sprawling megalopolis where you think twice about making any journey,' he says.

'The city has also become very expensive, but does not yet offer the facilities that you would expect in a major global city. Infrastructure planning and construction seem to be haphazard and knee-jerk. Public opinion is never consulted on major developments. And expats in Dubai are seen as nothing more than expendable "guest workers". Even if you buy property here you have no right to permanent residence and there is no possibility of becoming naturalised.'

On the other hand, Dubai, he says, has brought together a fascinating mixture of cultures and nationalities. The crime rate remains low and people feel safe walking anywhere. Keith's recommendation to anybody thinking of moving to the UAE is to make sure that the salary offered is adequate to cover expenses. 'Rented accommodation is staggeringly expensive. Also, if you have children, check out the schools and their fees – they can be crippling,' he says.

After 14 years, Keith decided he needed to take his family back to Europe. They are now living in Spain.

NEW ZEALAND

The attractions of New Zealand are obvious, not just thanks to the *Lord of the Rings* movies. The scenery really is stunning. Life's lived outdoors. People drive on the proper side of the road and speak English. The crime rate is low.

If there are downsides, these include the fact that it is the 'other side of the world' in every sense. There are jobs, but perhaps not enough variety if your intention is a career-boosting move. And there are people who wonder if the country's environmentally-conscious reputation is really the result of there not being enough people to do much damage.

QUICK FACTS

- **Land area:** 268,680 sq km
- **Population:** four million
- **Climate:** The New Zealand weather can catch Europeans by surprise. They know, of course, that because it's in the southern hemisphere the seasons are the opposite of Europe, with winter, for instance, from June to August. But the climate can also seem topsy-turvy, with the north being warmer than the south. And the differences are fairly extreme even though the country is generally described as 'temperate'. Parts of the south island inland can be as cold as −10° C in winter, while the far north is subtropical. The advantage of this varied weather is it allows New Zealanders to enjoy almost every type of sport, from skiing to sailing.
- **Language:** English
- **Currency:** New Zealand dollar (£1 = NZ$2.50, January 2008)
- **How long does it take to get there from the UK?** London to Auckland is 25 hours, to Wellington is 29 hours and to Christchurch is 30 hours.
- **How many British migrants are there?** 215,000 (about five per cent of the population)

- **Cost of living:** Unsurprisingly in a country that has traditionally been dominated by agriculture, local food is cheap. The economy has, however, been moving away from its reliance on lamb, butter and Kiwi fruit and there's a growing affluence in places such as Auckland. As a result you can enjoy a good standard of living on a salary that may seem low compared with Britain, provided you stick mostly to local products. But you can equally well enjoy an expensive lifestyle, if you insist on driving a Merc and surrounding yourself with top-of-the-range electronic goods.

THE ECONOMY

In the early 1980s, the New Zealand economy suffered something of a crisis when its concessionary access to British markets came to an end thanks to UK membership of the then EEC. It recovered well, developing into a more internationally competitive industrialised free market economy. Agricultural products continue to be the main exports.

The country exports an increasing amount to Australia. Its relations with other Pacific Rim countries meant it suffered in 1997 and 1998 as a result of the Asian economic crisis. This led to a rise in unemployment, but it has since fallen back to its historically low level of around 3.5 per cent.

Overall, the New Zealand economy is very stable. The biggest source of concern is the large current account deficit. And, of course, any country which is reliant on exports is vulnerable to the vicissitudes of world markets.

DOING BUSINESS IN NEW ZEALAND

The main thing to remember is that Kiwis are not Aussies. Mixing the two up will not make you popular. There's intense rivalry between the two countries, which finds its main expression on the sports field. It's *supposed* to be friendly, but when you see the Wallabies take on the All-Blacks at rugby, 'friendly' isn't the first word that springs to mind.

Generally New Zealanders are a little more reserved than Australians. It takes a little longer for them to open up, then they'll be friendly, humorous and sociable. They like people to be honest, direct and have a sense of humour. Any presentation you give should reflect this. Keep it brief as well.

It's not a bargaining culture either: negotiations should start from a realistic point. And don't make promises you can't keep. That'll be the end of a beautiful friendship.

WORK AND VISAS

There is a continuing skills shortage in New Zealand. That doesn't mean salaries are high, but it does mean you can get a visa if you meet the basic entry requirements.

This skilled migrant option is for suitably qualified people, aged 55 and under, who can 'add value' to New Zealand. It's based on a points system which you can calculate on the government's immigration website (www.immigration.govt.nz/pointsindicator). If you score over 100 points, you can submit an 'Expression of Interest'.

The first section of the points system indicator covers 'skilled employment', including both your formal qualifications and experience. It helps if you have qualifications in one of the areas of 'absolute skills shortage', which include everything from psychiatrists to electricians. For a full list, go to http://glossary.immigration.govt.nz/Areaofabsoluteskillsshortage.htm: the list is updated twice a year. Alternatively, you may be qualified in one of the areas identified for future growth. Currently these are, broadly, biotechnology, information/communications technology and the creative industries. It also helps if you already have a close relative living in New Zealand and your partner, if you have one, has skills and is proficient in English.

Another option is 'Work to Residence'. This is for people who are qualified in a highly specialised or in-demand field, or who have an exceptional talent in sports or the arts. The permit allows you to work temporarily in New Zealand as the first step towards gaining permanent residence, which you can apply for after two years. You also need a genuine offer of full-time, ongoing employment with a base salary of at least NZ$50,000 a year or sponsorship from a New Zealand arts, cultural or sporting organisation. You may also apply if you are offered employment in an occupation on the

Long Term Shortage Skill List. If you meet any of these criteria, you can fill in an application form online at the official immigration site.

Existing citizens and residents can sponsor their other family members to come and live in New Zealand. Those eligible include: partners, dependent children, parents and siblings of citizens or residents, even if they are grown up.

The country is also looking for enterprising people with a proven track record in business and the capacity to build, or invest in, new businesses and introduce new skills and technologies. There are a number of business migration options, the most common is the Long Term Business Visa (LTBV).

To be issued with an LTBV, you'll have to provide documentary evidence that you:

- have enough money to establish your business and make a viable contribution to the economy
- are suitably experienced and have not been involved with any business failures or fraud

Residence can applied for through an Entrepreneur Visa after the business has been running for two years. There is no age limit for this category, but for most other work visas you have to be 55 or under.

In 2007 the government introduced the 'Active Investor Migrant Category'. It has three tiers:

1. The top priority 'Global Investors', who have $20 million to invest and at least $5 million in active investment.

2. The second priority 'Professional Investors', who have $10 million to invest including at least $2 million actively, and 'General (Active) Investors' with a minimum of $2.5 million.

3. The last will be selected through a points system. There's a cap of 1,000 people to be admitted this way

STARTING A BUSINESS

Few countries are as enthusiastic as New Zealand about attracting immigrants to set up businesses. And the World Bank ranked New Zealand as the best of 155 countries for ease of doing business.

The country has had to overcome a fair amount of geographical adversity from being so isolated. It's also had to recover from the loss of its traditional UK market thanks to EU regulations. But much of the economic revival comes from the growth of small businesses and the government is keen to see that continue.

Small and medium enterprises (SMEs) are New Zealand's largest employers and they account for about 40 per cent of economic output. Most of these businesses employ less than five staff and very few have 20 or more.

Over a third of these SMEs are property and business service providers. Finance, insurance, personnel, construction, communication services and retail trade make up much of the balance. Tourism and IT are growing particularly fast. In fact if you're ever trying to think of the name of a Kiwi company which has become world-famous, look at Navman, a leading light in GPS satellite navigation systems which started in New Zealand before becoming part of a global multinational.

For Brits, there's a comfortable feel to company law which echoes that of the UK. You can set up as a sole trader, partnership or limited company. The amount of red tape involved is far less than in most countries and it's made particularly easy because just about everything is available for completion online.

The government also provides a wealth of information online for anybody considering starting a business from inside or outside New Zealand. Start by looking at www.business.govt.nz and www.immigration.govt.nz/migrant/stream/invest/startingabusiness.

PROPERTY AND ACCOMMODATION

Most New Zealanders own their homes and move frequently, so buying a place is fairly straightforward. It is, however, generally worth renting before buying so you get a clear idea of the market and where you really want to live.

The best property rental deals come from local papers. You really need to find out when the first editions hit the streets and be ready with your mobile phone, especially if you're looking in Auckland. The city's growing fast, but housing supply can't keep up with demand. There are websites, estate agents and relocation specialists that will find you property to rent, but beware of taking out long contracts from thousands of miles away – descriptions of flats, houses and their locations can be fairly inventive.

Once you've found somewhere, the rental process is fairly straightforward. The Department of Building and Housing (www.dbh.govt.nz) provides a standard agreement for landlords and tenants. Notice is 21 days for tenants and 90 days for landlords. And you're normally expected to pay a bond equal to one or two weeks' rent. This is held by a government department and repaid at the end of the tenancy, providing nothing has been broken.

The average price to rent an unfurnished three-bedroom property is around NZ$300 a week (June 2007), but you could easily pay twice as much for somewhere in an upmarket area of Auckland or Wellington, particularly if it's got a sea view. It'll also cost more if the tenancy is to be less than a year. Rents to some extent reflect the increasing price of homes across New Zealand which have boomed in recent years, although they're currently showing some signs of slowing down.

Most properties are sold through real estate agents who have to be registered. That doesn't mean you shouldn't haggle: it's quite acceptable to offer up to ten per cent below the asking price, although five per cent would perhaps be more normal. The property valuation company Quotable Value (www.qv.co.nz) is worth looking at before you make any sort of offer, as it provides a variety of statistics which will give you a clear idea of the going rate for the type of property you're after.

Compared with many countries, there are few legal pitfalls to beware of when buying property in New Zealand. The main thing to look out for is just how much it's going to cost to renovate the house that the real estate agent has told you is 'only in need of a little TLC'. Conveyancing may throw up a list of relatives with a claim to the property, and it's worth paying a lawyer to go through the procedure rather than doing it yourself.

If problems do arise, it's usually because the purchaser has been persuaded to act too fast. The agent may be telling the truth and there could be other potential buyers waiting in the wings, but that shouldn't stop you making sure your lawyer has inserted the appropriate clauses in the agreement to ensure that conditions are met. It's also worth ensuring your mortgage is agreed in principle before you start seriously looking for property. The purchase process can be very quick.

REPUBLIC OF SOUTH AFRICA (RSA)

There's much that's attractive about South Africa: the warm, dry climate would be regarded by many as perfect; the scenery's stunning; it's got a buoyant economy and there's a huge need for skilled workers and professionals. And English is spoken widely enough that you don't need to learn another language to get a job.

To balance against that, however, there's the deep legacy of apartheid, the profound division between the haves and have-nots. The separation is not strictly along race lines, but between the great mass of the unskilled, underpaid or unpaid population and the qualified, employed and comfortable minority. Move there and you'll join the haves, because they're the only people who can get a work permit.

At the same time, no discussion between people who have lived in South Africa can last more than two minutes without turning to the level of crime. It is undoubtedly high. The question you have to ask yourself is whether it's a price worth paying for the rest of the lifestyle.

QUICK DETAILS

- **Land area:** 1,219,912 square kilometres
- **Population:** 47 million (80 per cent black, nine per cent white, nine per cent 'coloured' or mixed race, two per cent Indian/Asian)
- **Climate:** The first thing to realise is that South Africa is in the southern hemisphere so, for instance, Christmas falls in the middle of summer. Rainfall is fairly low overall. It's also cooler than other countries on the same latitude, such as Australia, because of its altitude. Johannesburg, for instance, is around 1,700 metres above sea level which keeps average summer temperatures below 30 degrees Celsius, while in winter night-time temperatures can drop to freezing.

- **Main languages:** According to the 2001 census there are eight major languages: IsiZulu (first language of 23.8 per cent of the population), IsiXhosa (17.6 per cent), Afrikaans (13.3 per cent), Sepedi (9.4 per cent), English (8.2 per cent), Setswana (8.2 per cent), Sesotho (7.9 per cent) and Xitsonga (4.4 per cent).
- **Currency:** The South African Rand is a fairly volatile currency in world terms. It is, however, probably the most solid currency in Africa. As of January 2008, the rate was around 13 to the pound.
- **How long does it take to get there from the UK and are services year round?** A flight from London to Cape Town takes about eight hours, to Durban is just over 12 hours and to Johannesburg is a little more than 11 hours. Flights are year round. South Africa is two hours ahead of the UK.
- **How many British migrants are there and where do they live mostly?** There are an estimated 212,000 Britons in South Africa. Probably the biggest concentration is round Johannesburg, but you'll find English speakers all over the country.
- **Cost of living:** Generally, prices remain considerably lower than the UK despite inflation across the board. How cheap it seems depends partly on whether your savings and income are in pounds or rands, as well as what your taste is in luxury imported goods, which tend to be more expensive. More importantly, it depends on your family circumstances. Many expats choose to send their children to private schools which aren't cheap, but there are deep-rooted problems with the state education system.

THE ECONOMY

South Africa effectively has two economies, one of which is the match of most of Europe, and another that's impoverished and lacking many basic services. That doesn't stop the country having the most powerful economy in Africa, with a GDP representing about a quarter of the total for the whole continent. That includes 40 per cent of the continent's industrial output, 45 per cent of its mineral production and over half its electricity.

The country has a strong, modern and internationally highly regarded financial sector. The Johannesburg Stock Exchange is one of the world's top twenty exchanges by market capitalisation. The country's infrastructure of every type is the most developed in Africa.

Overall economic indicators are positive. Economic growth has averaged 3.5 per cent since the turn of the decade. At the same time inflation has turned downwards and the country's budget deficit has been reduced, largely, it seems, because of a rise in the number of registered taxpayers.

The IMF South Africa country report in 2005 said: 'The economy is now growing strongly, inflation has been lowered and has become more predictable, public finances have been strengthened, and the external position has improved markedly. The expansion in economic activity has created additional jobs.

'Given South Africa's position in the region, the country's strong economic performance has benefited the rest of Africa.'

The IMF warned, however, that that there were still serious economic challenges, including continuing high unemployment, poverty, wide disparities in wealth and a high incidence of HIV/Aids. But they came out in support of the South African authorities' approach to these problems, with policies aimed at raising economic growth in a stable economic environment and initiatives to reduce unemployment and improve social conditions.

DOING BUSINESS IN SOUTH AFRICA

Business people in South Africa look increasingly to America for their role models. That does not mean US-style informality is universal, though, so it's best to turn up for initial meetings at least dressed in a sober suit.

As in many other countries, networking is valuable in South Africa and the right introduction to a company can avoid a number of meetings with subordinates before you get to somebody capable of making a decision. And the best way of making conversation when networking is with an in-depth knowledge of sport, particularly rugby, cricket and football – especially the last, given that the country is to host the World Cup finals in 2010.

Perhaps the biggest issue for immigrants, however, is dealing with the multiplicity of ethnic groups, all of whom seem to have a different business culture. Even their ways of greeting vary, although fortunately a handshake with eye contact is the norm when they meet foreigners. It also seems to be generally the case that South Africans aren't big on haggling and would rather start with a realistic price. Deadlines, though, are more flexible.

JOBS AND WORK PERMITS

Work permits are only issued to people able to do a job where there is no suitably qualified South African. With unemployment estimated to be running in excess of 25 per cent, you might think that trying to find a suitable job would be a hopeless task for a foreigner. In fact, there's a huge skills shortage and it's getting worse.

A large part of the population missed out on education during the struggle to overthrow apartheid, creating an intrinsic problem that's been exacerbated since the end of white minority rule in 1993. The South African Institute of Race Relations estimates around 850,000 white people have left the country since 1995. Most of those who have departed are believed to be skilled workers aged between 20 and 40. At the same time, many qualified black South Africans, many of whom worked in the public sector, have also moved to other countries.

There is now such a shortage of skilled workers, particularly in the IT and finance sectors, that it threatens the rapid economic growth South Africa has enjoyed over the last decade. One effect of this is an increase in pay levels in the private sector in order to attract and retain employees. Salaries, however, generally compare poorly with those in Europe for equivalent jobs.

An added problem is the tight restriction on work permits and immigration. For instance, despite the types of skill where there's a shortage being well known, employers still always have to supply 'substantive proof that steps have been taken to ensure employment for SA citizens or permanent residents – for example, press clippings of advertisements placed for at least a month in national newspapers'.

You'll have to add that evidence to your application along with (among other things):

- proof of your qualification
- a CV

- testimonials from your previous employers
- police clearance certificates for all the countries you've lived in for more than a year
- a medical certificate
- an employment contract

It can be a slow process.

If you are issued with a work permit, you have to either make a cash deposit or obtain a bank guarantee for repatriation purposes. This is refundable when you leave South Africa. Work permits are valid for up to a year and are renewable.

STARTING A BUSINESS

It is South African government policy to support new business and overseas investment. There are plentiful financial incentives available across most sectors to encourage development.

The application process assumes that in order to set up a business you'll be making a long-term commitment to living in South Africa. A 12-month work permit wouldn't give you time to establish an enterprise, so instead you'll have to apply for permanent residence, a process that's meant to take between six months and a year, but frequently takes longer.

In order to be accepted, you have to provide evidence that you have sufficient funds to support yourself and your family during the set-up period. This could be regarded as three years or more depending on the type of business. You must transfer a minimum sum of money to South Africa in order to set up the business. The amount is determined by the Immigrants Selection Board (www.safrica.info/public_services/foreigners/immigration/immigration.htm).

A year after establishing your business, you have to provide audited financial statement to show that it is viable. You also have to prove that at least two South African citizens or permanent residents, excluding members of your family, have been and still are employed. Finally, you have to show the amount of money determined by the Immigrants Selection Board has been used for the intended purpose.

Although the application process is quite lengthy, it's perhaps less arduous than in some other countries. There are, however, some aspects of running a business in South Africa which can be fairly hard work. The Black Economic Empowerment (BEE) programme has introduced a number of measures to try and overcome the inequalities which have been carried over from the apartheid era. The legislative measures are mainly aimed at larger companies, which have to be at least partly owned and controlled by black citizens, although there is some leeway for multinationals with branches in South Africa. Smaller businesses may find they can't win state contracts or obtain grants if they're not BEE-compliant. It is, however, a programme which is still being developed, so consult a professional advisor and visit the extremely informative government website (www.southafrica.info) before making any decisions.

ACCOMMODATION AND PROPERTY

There's generally no shortage of rental properties except at the height of the holiday season and in the big cities. If you're planning to move to South Africa long term, it's probably best to do it in stages, starting with a short holiday rental, while you look for something longer term before deciding whether to buy.

Rentals are advertised in newspapers, magazines, websites and through estate agents. Rents are usually negotiable downwards, and a friendly agent may even tell you what you can get away with.

Once the rent has been agreed between you and the landlord, you have to sign a lease agreement under the Rental Housing Act. You then go round the property with the landlord and note any defects. Any deposit you pay has to be put into an interest-bearing account. At the end of the rental period, you go round the property again with the landlord and agree to any damages to be paid for out of the deposit. If there are none, the landlord has to refund your deposit, plus interest, within seven days. If there are repairs, the deposit is repaid within 14 days.

Property prices have risen by 300 per cent in the last decade. The average property is expected to hit the million rand mark in 2008 and first-time buyers are, understandably, now struggling to get on the property ladder.

To a British immigrant, however, paying £70–80,000 for a good-quality property seems a good deal. And compared to most African countries, the purchase process is pretty straightforward. That doesn't mean you should scrimp on buying the services of a good English-speaking lawyer, though.

Finance is a little more problematic. Overseas buyers are only allowed to borrow 50 per cent of the purchase price from South African banks. The local mortgage rates are, anyway, very high at around 12.5 per cent. At the same time, British financial institutions are somewhat reluctant to lend on properties in South Africa. Despite this, prices are expected to keep rising fast until at least the 2010 World Cup. The potential for non-residents to make money from property is reduced by capital gains tax, which is collected on the basis of adding 25 per cent of the profit to the seller's annual earnings and charging according to the standard income tax rate of up to 40 per cent.

USA

Gone are the days when the United States could say: 'Give me your tired, your poor, your huddled masses yearning to breathe free,' as the inscription on the Statue of Liberty reads. The US has plenty of poor, huddled masses of its own. It wants the bright, the highly skilled, ready to join its growing knowledge industries.

If you have those qualities there's probably no better place in the world to develop them. There's a constant demand for skilled, professional workers, although you'll need to go through the bureaucratic hoops necessary to get a work permit.

QUICK FACTS

- **Land area:** 9.8 million square kilometres
- **Population:** 298 million (July 2006 estimated)
- **Climate:** Most of the country is temperate, although the differences between winter and summer may be far more extreme than in the UK. Hawaii and Florida are tropical and Alaska is arctic.
- **Main languages:** English is the principal language for a little over 80 per cent of the population, while Spanish is first tongue of more than ten per cent of Americans and is the most widely taught second language in the United States. An assortment of other languages (such as French, Hawaiian and the Native American languages) account for the rest.
- **Currency:** US dollar (£1 = $1.95, January 2008)
- **How long does it take to get there from the UK and are services year round?** Flight times vary between roughly seven hours from London to New York or 11 hours from London to Los Angeles.
- **How many British migrants are there and where do they live mostly?** There are 678,000 Brits in the United States, with concentrations in eastern cities such as New York and Boston, on the west coast in Los Angeles and San Francisco. More recently, many have bought homes in Florida.

- **Cost of living:** There are enormous variations even within the USA. To enjoy the same standard of living in New York City as, for instance, in Alabama would require twice the income. Accommodation charges are obviously the biggest single factor, but almost everything costs more. And there's a greater selection of things to spend your money on. Across the USA as a whole, most goods and services are generally cheaper than in the UK. But it all depends on what you can earn.

THE ECONOMY

It is impossible to exaggerate the global importance of the US economy. It is, of course, the biggest by gross domestic product, but it's also the largest importer and one of the three largest exporters. New York is the world's leading financial centre.

Other countries have faster rates of growth, but that's arguably because they are starting from a lower base. The US rate of growth has, however, remained sustainably high with low rates of unemployment and inflation. There are concerns about high levels of consumer, national and external debt along with rising economic disparities and inequalities in the healthcare system.

One of the key strengths of the US economy has been the continuing high expenditure on research and development. This has helped keep the country at the forefront of electronics, IT and other advanced technology. At the same time, it has exported much of its manufacturing to China, leading to a massive deficit to that country.

DOING BUSINESS IN THE USA

Most countries have a fairly standard basic etiquette which extends across different industries, with some variations of course. Viewed from outside the US, business interactions can seem to be almost totally casual. That's far from the reality.

Yes, technology companies in California make a virtue of informality. The CEO might turn up at a meeting in a T-shirt and shorts. But on the other coast, New York bankers are as conservative as they come. Those are the extremes. It's the points in between, geographically and sartorially, that pose the challenge for anybody doing business or job hunting.

So how do you decide what the level of formality is likely to be for your first meeting? For a start, the type of business will give you a clue. Lawyers and bankers, for instance, will be conservative. Look at the company's website, where there will probably be pictures of the executives. Take a cue from those. As a general rule of thumb, try to dress one step above your hosts. If website portraits show them in T-shirts, wear an open-neck shirt. If they're in open neck shirts, put on a tie. Women should wear a skirt or dress. Don't worry, they'll expect a Brit to be slightly stuck-up and it's better to be slightly over-dressed than be way too informal.

Dress concerns aside, the reality of business meetings will differ little from anywhere else, although Americans may be less deferential as far as seniority is concerned. Politeness, a firm handshake and eye contact are universal.

The other thing that's still fairly universal is the role of the motor car as status symbol. Just watch your T-shirted CEO leave the meeting in his Ferrari, Porsche or BMW. So don't hire the cheapest vehicle on the rental company's books: pay a little bit more. A picture of you squeezing into a tiny Korean car is not the image you want to leave with your potential business partners.

JOBS AND VISAS

The Holy Grail for anybody wanting to move permanently to the US is the 'Green Card'. This is a little confusing because the United States Permanent Resident Card - or form I-551, to use its official title - is not actually green and hasn't been for over 30 years. Nonetheless the name has persisted.

It is an identification card proving that an individual is a 'lawful permanent resident' of the USA and thus may live and work there. They must maintain their residence and may be removed, usually as the result of a criminal conviction.

The almost mythical status of the green card attracts more magazine and Web con artists than you can click a mouse at. The biggest target for the scammers is the so-called 'Green Card Lottery'. The conmen give the impression that if you pay them up to $250, they can somehow improve you chances of winning a resident card. It's nonsense, of course.

In reality, you've probably got no chance of winning. That's because the lottery is part of the Diversity Visa program which sees about 50,000 immigrant visas made available to people born in countries with low rates of immigration to the USA. 'Low' generally means less than 50,000 in the last five years. Even with this proviso, there are millions of applicants. Those selected – the winners – are given the opportunity to apply for permanent residence along with their spouses and children.

Fortunately, the lottery isn't the only way to get a Green Card. The rules and procedures do change, however, on a fairly frequent basis. The best source of information is the issuing body, the US Citizenship and Immigration Services (USCIS) and its website (www.unitedstatesvisas.gov), which is part of the Department of Homeland Security. Not every other website offering information is a scam, but many are out of date.

Usually you have to go through a three-stage process to get a Green Card. It can take several years, depending on the country of birth and immigrant category. The stages are:

1. **Immigrant Petition.** A relative or employer petitions the USCIS on your behalf.

2. **Waiting List.** There are quotas for just about every type of immigrant visa and most people who have been successful with their petition are put on a lengthy waiting list. The only real exceptions are the immediate relatives of US citizens, but not relatives of people holding Green Cards. They've got their own hoops to jump through.

3. **Immigrant Visa Adjudication.** Once a visa number becomes available, the applicant must either apply to the USCIS to adjust their current status to permanent resident or apply for an immigrant visa at a US consulate.

Most British would-be immigrants look for an employer to sponsor them and petition the USCIS. This means proving that there is no US citizen or Green Card holder who could do that same job.

There are a number of employment-based (EB) categories, the top two of which, EB1 and EB2, may receive a waiver. EB1 covers priority workers: those with extraordinary ability in sciences, arts, education, business or athletics, or outstanding professors and researchers. EB2 includes: professionals holding advanced degrees (PhD, master's degree, or at least five years of progressive post-baccalaureate experience) or persons of exceptional ability in sciences, arts or business. The most popular, however, is EB3: skilled workers, professionals and other workers. Once a petition is approved, it is then a matter of waiting until a visa becomes available which may take some time.

You can also be employed in the United States if you have a work permit, or Employment Authorization Document, to use its official title. These have to be renewed every year and are actually only applicable to a fairly limited group of people, such as asylum seekers, students and applicants for permanent residence status.

More common is the H-1B visa, which allows US employers to hire skilled foreign workers on a temporary basis. Many of the employees work for high-tech corporations and a large proportion come from the Indian subcontinent. Currently the maximum period a person may have H-1B status is six years, unless the employer is a defence contractor in which case this may be extended to ten years. People working on an H-1B visa may apply for a Green Card while they're living in the USA. They can also bring their spouses at any time, although their spouses don't automatically receive a visa that entitles them to work.

Further categories of visa are the L-1, which is given to people working for an international company with a US branch, and the O-1 visa which is for 'Aliens of Extraordinary Ability' from the field of science, education, business or athletics. It means 'a level of expertise indicating that the person is one of the small percentage who have arisen to the very top of the field of endeavour'. Well, that's not me.

Given the difficulty and complexity of getting an appropriate visa, many foreigners simply opt to work illegally. There are literally millions of them. The common image is of people from developing countries employed as domestics, in catering or agriculture. But it also includes people in better-paid white-collar occupations, even though it's just as illegal for them.

To be paid in anything other than cash in hand in the United States requires a social security number. There's a lucrative trade in forged documentation for this, some of which is high quality and priced to match. There are strict penalties for those knowingly using forgeries: you may be fined, deported and permanently refused re-admission.

STARTING A BUSINESS

Unless you have a substantial amount of money to invest, it's unlikely you'll get a visa to set up a business. Once you've got your Green Card, though, you should find the process fairly straightforward. Making a fortune as your own boss is, however, a popular version of the American Dream and you'll probably face intense competition.

If you're planning to start your business from home, the first thing is to check local and state licensing and zoning regulations. The local zoning office can tell you how regulations in your area may affect your business plans. These vary enormously from state to state and even county to county. Certain types of business may not be allowed, particularly in residential zones. There may be restrictions on parking, the size of signs and the hours you can operate.

See if your business requires any licences and file the necessary forms before you start trading. The most likely one is a sellers' or resale permit if you're selling something and there's a sales tax in the state.

If you operate as a sole trader and don't have any employees, you can use your Social Security number as a tax ID. You may find an accountant is useful to help keep your books in order, especially while you're getting used to a new system, but there are a number of good software packages which will take you through the process of producing a filing for the IRS (Internal Revenue Service, the US equivalent of HM Revenue and Customs) step by step. The important point is to keep your books up to date from the start and not wait until just before the tax deadline.

You'll probably have to register the name of your business, unless your own surname's included. The process is known as DBA or 'doing business as'. To do this, usually you go along to the county clerk, register the name, then, for the legal record, run an advertisement in four issues of your local paper. This registration is not just a legal requirement: your bank probably won't cash any cheques made out to your business without it.

There are plenty of useful websites, including that of the US Chamber of Commerce which has a toolkit for people planning to start a business (www.uschamber.com). The US Government also provides a substantial number of resources at www.business.gov.

ACCOMMODATION AND PROPERTY

The chances are that you'll at least start off in rented accommodation. There are enormous variations in price and availability according to area. The hardest places to find apartments are probably New York, Los Angeles and San Francisco. And now's the time you find out just how regulated living in America can be.

The actual process of hunting is fairly simple, if somewhat time consuming. Increasingly properties are advertised online through websites such as www.craigslist.org, which covers most of the US cities. Even if you're pressed for time, it's always best for you to visit places before you sign the rental agreement (it's a big decision to make based on a slightly grainy photograph), so it's a good idea to plan to stay in a hotel for a couple of weeks while you look.

Once you've found somewhere, probably with a minimum one-year lease, it can get slightly complicated. Your landlord will want to see your credit report. This is based on your credit history, how good you've been at paying back money you've borrowed on credit cards, loans and so on. If you haven't been living in the USA, of course, you won't have much of a history. All you can do is provide a covering letter explaining why you don't have a high score on your report. And it is worth opening an account at a major US bank as soon as you can so that you start building up a history.

Next, you'll sign a lease which may well be fairly detailed. The landlord will probably ask for one or two months' rent as a security deposit which, in many states, will be held in an account which will pay you interest. You should inspect the property with your landlord and note any damage before paying this deposit so that you're not held responsible for it when you come to leave.

What may seem unusual to Europeans is that there's quite likely to be a set of building rules which apply to every resident. These may include items such as times when excessive noise is prohibited and whose responsibility it is to ensure communal areas are cleaned. Breaking these rules may be grounds for terminating your lease.

Buying a property is not dramatically different from the UK (http://money.howstuffworks.com/house-buying11.htm) and there is the advantage compared with other foreign countries that you'll be speaking approximately the same language as your 'realtor' ('estate agent', as we'd say).

It is worth going to a lender to get your home loan or mortgage pre-qualified. If you've only recently arrived in the US, this won't be an easy exercise, especially after the economic woes caused by sub-prime lending in the summer of 2007. Still, the lender wants your business and the process should give you a reasonable idea of what you can afford. And it doesn't cost you anything.

When you do find the home of your dreams, or at least something you can live with until you can afford the home of your dreams, you will be faced with a series of extra costs on top of the purchase price. There'll be the deposit of between five and 20 per cent of the price; two or three months' property tax; a year's house insurance; lawyers' bills and so on, which will add between two and seven per cent to the agreed price.

BANKING

As it's become simpler to move to many countries to live and work, it's also become easier to allow savings and pension plans to become something of a mess. This can lead to missed tax breaks or even financial penalties. Before making a move, be sure to consult an independent financial advisor with expertise in expatriate savings and international tax planning.

Don't think, by the way, that you should ignore this advice simply because you're going abroad to 'test the water'. That's how many of us start and it can be remarkably hard to sort out what you've left behind. The first step is to ensure that the tax authorities recognise that you are no longer resident (see pp. 142–45).

OFFSHORE ACCOUNTS

Once your non-resident status is confirmed, you should investigate placing your savings offshore. This may conjure images of billionaire tax-dodgers, but it's generally just a way of ensuring the revenue doesn't make automatic deductions while you're abroad. It also avoids the situation where you earn and pay tax on money in one country then get taxed again when you send it back to the UK.

One important change to note is that since the introduction of the European savings tax directive in 2006, savers resident in the EU with accounts in Guernsey, Jersey and the Isle of Man no longer automatically see their interest paid before tax.

There's nothing illegal about an offshore bank account unless you're using it to conceal activities from the police, tax authorities or creditors. Many of the bank names will be familiar from Britain's high streets. They also operate frequently from places that can seem more British than Britain, such as the Channel Islands and the Isle of Man.

They also offer much the same facilities as UK banks, including cheques, credit and debit cards, Internet banking and so on. There is a certain amount of bureaucracy involved in opening an account. This is as a result of the international laws on money laundering introduced to curb terrorism and drug trafficking.

Generally, it's easier to go through this process before moving abroad as it involves producing proof of identity and address in the form of a passport, utility bills, driving licence and so on. If the offshore account is with a UK bank, this is generally just a matter of popping into a branch where the documents will be checked before copies are signed and stamped.

It's possible to do the same thing abroad, except it's less likely there will be a branch of the UK bank nearby. The alternative is to get photocopies of the paperwork officially certified by the likes of an international bank, consular official or lawyer. From my experience this is not quite as quick, simple or cheap as it could be.

It is worth shopping around to find the bank that offers the best rates and the best service. Things to look out for are the availability of 24-hour customer service and Internet banking. The former is particularly important if you're working in a different time zone from the bank.

Although your offshore bank may be a subsidiary of a big name from the British high street, you should be aware that you won't be covered by the UK financial services compensation scheme. Well-known institutions do, however, have a reputation to protect.

Although offshore banking is useful, you'll almost certainly need an account with a local bank in your new country. The very least you'll need it for is to set up standing orders for your utility bills. Fortunately, in most countries, you simply need to turn up with your passport and a small initial deposit to start your account.

CHOOSING THE RIGHT BANK

What is considerably more difficult is to decide which bank to join. In many countries, you'll find that simply having money in you account is not enough to stop bank charges. There can be deductions for all sorts of items. It was a shock, for instance, the first time I was charged for putting money into my account. Banks may also be responsible for ensuring some government taxes are paid, so you can find an unexpected amount suddenly withheld from your account, particularly when buying property, with the difference being repaid some months later.

It may be worth asking around or visiting expat websites to see which banks are recommended by the people who have used them. The trouble is that the differences between banks internationally tend to be as opaque as they are in the UK and account holders aren't usually too sure whether the problems they're having are specific to their bank or general.

It is, however, worth querying bank charges. It's often the case overseas that local bank managers have far more autonomy than those in the UK, and they may be able to reduce or even write off charges. Of course, they may not. But, if you don't ask, you don't get.

The next thing to consider is how you get your money from the UK into your account overseas. Even if it's just 'start-up' money to cover rent, deposits and initial living expenses, the amounts to be transferred will run into thousands of pounds. Buying property abroad will probably push this up into the hundreds of thousands.

The simplest, but very expensive, way of transferring cash is simply to ask your British high street bank, probably without checking the small print to see how much it costs. You'll probably be charged commission of 2 per cent and transfer fees ranging from £20 to £40 for each transaction.

Often, the overseas transfer is carried out at the tourist exchange rate, which is two or three per cent below the commercial rate. If you were transferring the money from the UK to buy an overseas property costing €150,000 it would probably cost around £5,000 more to use a high street bank instead of going through a specialist foreign exchange broker (see p. 195).

Incidentally, setting up a foreign exchange or 'forex' trading account is best done *before* you leave the UK. There are a number of forms that need to be filled in and checks to be carried out as a result of international legislation to prevent money laundering. This is far more straightforward if you're in Britain. Once you've opened one or more accounts, there is no obligation to use them and the forms don't take long to complete.

Once you've opened your foreign exchange account, the process of transferring the money is almost scarily simple. You just phone up your foreign exchange dealer who will then make an offer based on the current spot price of the currency. Either you accept it or you try another company. Once agreed on the phone, you have a binding contract to pay the forex company.

A few minutes later you'll receive an e-mail confirming the deal with one form for you to sign and another to fill in with details of the foreign bank that's to receive the funds. You can either post, fax or scan and attach the completed forms to an e-mail.

Finally, you have to ensure that the foreign exchange dealers receive your pounds sterling. With most British banks, this process can be carried out over the phone or on the Internet. There may be costs involved, depending on the amount involved and the speed of the transfer. But, providing you make the payment to the foreign exchange company within the agreed period, the amount of foreign currency you receive will be fixed at the point you made the initial phone call and agreed the price.

If you're transferring a substantial amount of money overseas, for instance to buy a property, the process can turn you into something of an international exchange speculator. Prices on the money markets rise and fall by the minute. If you're sending £100,000 to a European Union country and the pound gains a cent against the euro, you've instantly gained 1,000 euros. At the time of writing, that's worth about £700. It's better than working for a living.

Of course, the opposite can happen just as easily. If you're worried about foreign exchange fluctuations, a specialist broker such as Moneycorp can help out by agreeing a fixed rate for future payments. This is particularly useful if you're buying a new property overseas where there are regular amounts to be paid to the builder during the construction. You can also make similar fixed-rate arrangements for monthly transfers from the UK, which is useful if you still have rental income or investments in Britain.

USEFUL WEBSITES

There's almost too much information at www.lowtax.net, but its comprehensive and regularly updated coverage of the world's offshore centres is hard to beat.

To compare rates for thousands of types of offshore accounts try www.moneyfacts.co.uk or www.interest-rates.org.uk.

For an exhaustive list of the world's offshore banks, visit: www.worldoffshorebanks.com.

INCOME TAX

Some readers of a certain age may remember the Rolling Stones heading off into tax exile on the Riviera. As a teenager, I thought they had achieved the perfect combination of sun, debauchery and economy. But much has changed since the 1960s, not least Britain's position as one of the higher tax economies. In fact, London now provides a haven for many of the super-rich from other countries.

There may still be tax advantages to be had from moving abroad, but it depends where you go, what you're going to be doing and how long you're going to be away from the UK. With a few exceptions, notably those countries such as the United Arab Emirates or Saudi Arabia which have a zero tax regime, it's very hard to make comparisons. Even within the European Union states not only have very different rates of taxation, but they also vary widely in the way tax is assessed.

The Stones' old stomping ground, France, for instance, appears to squeeze high earners hard. Tax there, however, is assessed by dividing the income by the number of people in the household, which often means a family ends up paying less than they would elsewhere. And France recently lowered its punitive top rate – and under the Sarkozy government taxation is likely to fall further.

But before you even start to look at rates for different countries, you need to work out *where* you're going to have to pay your tax. A 'digital nomad' might be developing software in Spain for companies in the UK. So which country gets the income tax?

'Most countries have a 183-day rule, which defines where you are resident for tax purposes,' explains Ross Mackenzie, tax partner with international accountants Mazars. 'You don't pay the tax where it's earned, but where you live or your "centre of economic interest", as the tax authorities call it.'

Your residency status in other countries is irrelevant as far as your UK tax residency is concerned. To be tax resident in the UK, you must be physically present in the UK for at least 183 days of the current tax year.

If for four consecutive tax years you visit the UK, for any reason, and the visits average more than 90 days per year, you will be classed as resident from the start of the fifth year. If you come to the UK intending to spend more than 90 days a year in the country, you'll be treated as resident from the day of arrival. If you plan to work in Britain for at least two years, you'll be treated as resident from the day you arrive in the country.

It sounds simple. You basically pay your tax where you live for most of the year. Well, it might be straightforward if Pitt the younger hadn't introduced income tax to Britain a couple of centuries ago using a variation on the mediaeval fiscal calendar. So, while most other countries measure liabilities ending on 31 December, Britain's year runs to 5 April. 'Some people try to use that difference to their advantage,' Mackenzie says. In other words, they can claim allowances for both countries.

But, although it may theoretically be possible to receive two sets of tax allowances, it's not easy. HM Revenue and Customs (HMRC, which incorporates the old Inland Revenue) requires a considerable amount of evidence that one of its tax payers really has departed its shores. The department does, however, provide detailed information in booklet form and on its website at www.hmrc.gov.uk.

It may sound obvious, but don't begin to think that because the tax authorities have accepted the fact that you've set up home in another country you can overlook the need to register in this new jurisidiction. You may be gone, but you're not forgotten. Many people spend time working abroad for occasional periods without leaving Britain permanently.

If most of your time is spent in the UK, that's your 'ordinary residence'. The phrase refers to the longer term and is based on your usual or 'habitual' place of residence rather than where you're resident in a specific tax year. So you can be *ordinarily* resident in the UK, even you are no longer resident.

Of course there has to be a time limit and HMRC usually examines your ordinary residence over a three-year period. If you've been non-resident for three full tax years, you'll probably be considered to be not ordinarily resident in the UK.

This can catch out the unwary. I know somebody who was working as cabin crew for several airlines and moved to Spain. As she was in another

European Union country, she didn't need a work permit and she didn't get round to filling in the tax forms either. Then she got hit with a massive bill for three years of back taxes, fines and interest.

Most countries have 'double taxation' agreements with each other. These ensure that individuals are not taxed twice on the same income. Unfortunately, that doesn't mean you can choose to pay tax to the regime with the lowest rates. You're also liable to British income tax on investment income from UK sources. This includes interest income, dividends and rental income.

Interest income received in the UK would normally have tax deducted at source at a rate of 20 per cent. For complete tax years of non-residence, you can ask to have this income paid gross which would be taken into account when calculating your tax liability.

Dividends from UK companies will always be paid net of a withholding tax collected at source. This counts as a tax credit and can be used to meet all or part of your tax bill. You can't reclaim the tax credit, however, if you do not owe any tax.

Any profit from renting out a UK property will be liable to UK tax. There are fortunately a fair number of expenses that are deductible from rental income, such as maintenance costs, management fees and mortgage interest.

There is an additional point to be considered, which is where you are 'domiciled'. This is not the same as your centre of economic interest and, indeed, you can be living outside the UK for decades, but still technically be domiciled here. This mostly affects inheritance tax so it is considered in greater detail in the next chapter.

Although tax is subject to political vagaries, an accountant will be able to make a reasonable assessment of liabilities according to the laws of your intended country of domicile. But accountancy is an art, not a science, and legislation does not always reflect varying national attitudes to tax authorities. Sometimes the declaration of income is regarded effectively as 'voluntary' or at least 'as little as you can get away with and not get investigated by the authorities'.

A common Mediterranean attitude is: 'Which do you love more, the state or your family? So why should you give more than is necessary to the state?'

In many places, and for obvious reasons I'm not going to be too specific, avoidance is effectively built into the system. It is, for instance, still quite common in rural areas for property and other major purchases to involve a substantial amount of 'black money' ". Perhaps a third of the actual price of a property may be handed over to the vendor in cash and never declared to the authorities.

As a result, it was suggested that the mini economic boom in the run-up to the introduction of the euro was caused by people rushing to spend their undeclared pesetas, lira and escudos before they became worthless. It also explains something that had baffled me. I couldn't understand why the large hardware store near where I live in Ibiza has the biggest selection of safes I have ever seen. Obviously some are for tourist hotels and apartments, but many look big and secure enough to store the cash and crown jewels of a small sovereign nation rather than a holidaymaker's papers and trinkets.

INHERITANCE TAX

As Benjamin Franklin said: 'Certainty? In this world nothing is certain but death and taxes.' Inheritance tax (IHT) neatly brings the two certainties together. The reason for devoting a separate section to IHT is that the British government's inheritance tax tentacles stretch further than for any other form of tax.

Almost all other taxation is based on which country you are defined as being resident in that year. Although movement across borders obviously has an effect, broadly speaking if you are out of the UK for more than 183 days you aren't resident. You may, however, be treated as 'ordinarily resident' for tax purposes if you spend more than 91 days a year in Britain over a period of four years.

IHT, however, is based on 'domicile', a somewhat complex legal term. Usually it's the country on your passport and it's hard to change. If you've been resident in the UK for 17 of the last 20 years, you are deemed to be domiciled for IHT purposes. That means your successors are liable for IHT on all your assets worldwide.

It is possible to persuade the UK tax authorities that you have renounced all ties with the country, but this normally means you have no bank accounts, property or club memberships. Even ownership of a burial plot is sufficient to prevent you changing domicile as it signals an intention to return. Benjamin Franklin would have been proud.

Even if all the hoops have been gone through and the authorities are satisfied that you are domiciled abroad, IHT will still be due on any UK assets. Recent changes mean that both spouses have an allowance currently of £300,000 each which can be combined. Although this adds a whole new layer of complexity where divorce and remarriage are involved it will reduce the number of estates liable for IHT. But it will still leave a substantial number of people looking for ways to reduce the burden of IHT.

Changing domicile can mean paying more in IHT. Although most countries have dual-taxation agreements with the UK to ensure, broadly, that you don't pay tax twice on the same income, only a very few of these agreements mention IHT specifically. In other words, your successors could be taxed twice. And even if they had the option to choose in which country to pay the tax, the UK looks cheap in comparison with some regimes.

As is probably abundantly clear already, this is an area where you should take expert advice, preferably both in the UK and in your new country of residence. You should certainly have a will which covers any country which might have a claim on your assets following your death. Dying without a will, or 'intestate' in the legal jargon, can even leave a surviving spouse with a substantial bill.

Making a will is, anyway, the starting point of 'estate planning' which can help ensure that your worldly possessions are passed on to the people of your choice, rather than the tax authorities. The best-known way of doing this is through gifts. Up to £3,000 a year is tax exempt. More than that is potentially exempt, in that no tax is due provided you survive seven years beyond making the gift. There's a sliding scale of liability should you not live for the full seven years.

More complex methods exist, including 'Nil Rate Band' trusts which are intended to put all or at least part of your wealth beyond the reach of the tax authorities. However, this is very much a matter of professional advice and you should investigate using a member of the Society of Trust and Estate Practitioners (STEP). The society has a website at www.step.org. The rules governing trusts are complex and subject to fairly frequent change.

As an expatriate you'll have to see a will as a work in progress, subject to changes in both your circumstances and regulations. Moving across borders will add one set of complications. Marriage can create another. It's not uncommon now for partners to be domiciled in two different countries and resident in a third, which could necessitate writing three co-ordinated wills. Without the right paperwork the surviving spouse in some countries such as Spain may be liable for IHT on family property or be forced to pass it on to undeserving children.

Although it can sound horribly complicated, it needn't be. Drawing up a will and getting the right legal advice isn't difficult. The independent

Society of Will Writers has plenty of background on its website (www.thesocietyofwillwriters.co.uk). Will Aid is supported by solicitors who give their services for free to raise money for charity every year. Its website (www.willaid.org) is also a mine of information. But if it's left to your heirs to deal with, it can be both highly expensive and extremely time consuming. Check out any major queries with HMRC, so that you can be sure you're up to date with all relevant legislation.

INSURANCE

Nobody likes buying insurance. It feels too much as if you're expecting something to go wrong. And unfortunately medical cover is anything but simple. In the jargon of the industry, policies are 'very flexible'. This means that, unlike a car where you have the choice of a couple of levels of cover and a few extras, with medical insurance you can change everything, including items you've almost certainly never thought of.

You will have to spend some time with a broker if you're buying the insurance yourself or going through the fine print on a policy your employer's bought for you. There's a very obvious wrong moment to discover that the cover's not what you expected.

The first thing to check is that you and your family, if they're part of the policy, will be covered wherever you are. If work takes you to many countries you'll need cover that takes account of that. Don't forget that if you're no longer resident in the UK you'll no longer automatically receive free treatment.

If you're still resident within the European Union you're entitled to a European Health Identity Card (EHIC) which gives you the right to the same national health treatment as locals on short trips to other EU countries and Switzerland. The key phrase is 'short trips', which generally means less than three months. It's not valid if you've moved somewhere to live.

If you start paying tax and national insurance in a new country, you'll be entitled to cover under its health service. There are also reciprocal agreements with many countries so that for shorter periods abroad, although you'll be paying UK national insurance contributions, you'll be entitled to cover in your country of temporary residence. You can find details of these agreements on the UK Revenue and Customs website (www.hmrc.gov.uk).

Although you may be entitled to basic care, this can be little more than a safety net. Private health insurance will cover more, but it's deciding how much more that makes the process of choosing and checking a policy so complex.

The most basic plans cover in-patient treatment, which includes the medical fees, hospital accommodation charges and, generally, road ambulance hire. What it may not cover are items such as at-home nursing, day care treatment and emergency evacuation. The last is particularly important in countries with poor standards of healthcare where you may even need to be flown across borders to get the proper level of treatment.

More expensive policies incorporate out-patient cover, which may include consultations with GPs and other medical practitioners as well as medical check-ups. Most have a maximum annual limit on how much can be spent on such preventive treatment.

Policies also vary on how much freedom you are given to choose the doctor, hospital or clinic that treats you. Some will only reimburse you if you use one of the facilities on their list, which may be quite limited.

If you or your spouse could become pregnant, you should ensure that maternity cover is included. There is always a waiting period before you can make any claims. As well as the costs of birth you should ensure there is cover for congenital defects which can be very expensive.

Incidentally, you should check that the policy generally has a very high ceiling for the amount you are able to claim, particularly if it covers the United States. Most are $1–2 million annually or $5 million for the life of a policy. These sums should be adequate even for organ transplants, but you should question any limits which are considerably lower.

Most policies have a long list of exclusions, some of which are obvious such as cosmetic surgery – breast enhancements do seem an unlikely insurance benefit. Others are more controversial. HIV/Aids treatment is generally covered only if it can be proved that it was caught through a medical procedure, such as a blood transfusion. Another area which insurers are looking at is acts of terrorism. Generally, innocent bystanders are covered, but check the exact wording on the policy. The same applies if you participate in just about any sport more active than snooker. Exclusions are not limited to skiing and mountaineering, but often include rugby and football.

A common way of keeping premium costs down is through 'deductibles' or an 'excess'. The policy holder would be expected to pay the first, say, £30 for any treatment. The sum may be calculated annually, in which case the insurance company would pay all the charges once an agreed threshold had been passed. Another variation is 'co-paying' where the policy holder would pay an agreed percentage of, say, dentistry charges. There are even policies that offer a no-claims discount.

Any policy you take out should be guaranteed to be automatically renewable. This is very important because if you do develop any sort of chronic illness, you may have a need for continuing treatment beyond the life of the existing policy. Finding a different one could be difficult. Insurance companies will generally exclude new clients' 'pre-existing conditions' from cover.

If, however, you do already have an ongoing health problem, shop around. You might be rejected by the first company you approach, but that doesn't mean they'll all turn you down. Most will set a time limit before paying for treatment of pre-existing conditions and load the premium, but at least you'll have cover if anything else happens.

Do not, by the way, be tempted to 'forget' about a chronic condition when applying for insurance. You may not be found out, but if you are, it will be at the worst possible moment when you're seeking medical treatment. Incidentally, lack of cover for pre-existing medical conditions generally includes everything that pre-dates the start of the policy, even if it hadn't been diagnosed.

Having ensured you have got automatically renewable cover, do not allow your policy to lapse, perhaps because you've changed address, started using a new credit card or moved your bank account. If your account isn't paid up and you develop a long-term illness, finding an insurer is likely to be, at best, very expensive.

This also shows why it is so important that you get the right insurer and policy from the start. It's not difficult to change while you're young and in good health. As you get older or begin to suffer lasting health problems, moving to a new insurer or changing your level of cover is not so easy.

That is something you should also bear in mind when deciding in which country to buy your insurance. If you've moved to a new country permanently then there may be advantages to buying medical insurance there. Policies should be geared to the local health system that everybody has to deal with.

You also won't be paying for perhaps unnecessary cover and for the services of an English-speaking broker.

Of course if you already have private health insurance in the UK, it's worth approaching your provider to see if you can get your cover extended internationally. This may even be possible if you are planning to be self-employed when you leave Britain after being part of a company scheme.

ADDITIONAL INSURANCE

Life insurance and critical illness cover

You may already have life cover which will pay out a lump sum if you die. Check that any policies you have are still valid if you move abroad. There's a good chance they won't be.

It's also the case that you're far more likely to suffer from a debilitating illness or disability than you are to die before you are 65. Critical illness cover provides an income if you are permanently disabled or are diagnosed with a specific illness. As ever, there are a wide variety of policies available offering different benefits, some of which combine life insurance with critical illness cover.

Kidnapping insurance

In some places such as parts of South America, Russia and the Middle East, kidnapping is a serious problem. It is possible to get insurance to pay ransom demands, but the premiums run into thousands of pounds a year. Some organisations do pay for cover, if only out of self-interest - recruiting employees could be difficult if they feel they might be abandoned if the worst should happen.

Car insurance

If you're taking a car abroad, your British insurance is valid in many countries for at least minimum third-party cover for several months. At the same time, you'll probably have to register the car locally, a process which in many countries can be time-consuming and quite expensive.

Whether insuring your re-registered British car or a locally bought one, you'll need to buy insurance locally as well. In countries with a large expat community, there are usually English-speaking brokers. Some are good, but others may trade on your language difficulties and won't get you the best deal. Ask around and try and find people who've had experience of them, especially if they've had to claim.

An alternative is to check on the Web. As in Britain, many of the large insurers are represented online and even offer a discount for buying that way. It's best if you've got a friend who speaks the local language well. Find out exactly what everything means before you commit yourself. It can be hard enough to understand the small print on policies which are (allegedly) in English.

HEALTH INSURANCE CHECKLIST

Not all health insurance policies are created equal. As you go through yours, pay particular attention to the following areas:

- **Sports.** Many policies exclude injuries arising from activities such as skiing, diving and climbing. Others are rather broader and may include riding, rugby and hockey, for example. If you take part in any physical activity, make sure it is not excluded.
- **International travel.** Make sure cover is not restricted to just your country of residence, or ensure you have adequate travel insurance if you're away. And that includes time spent in the UK.
- **Pre-existing conditions.** It may be very difficult to find cover for ongoing health problems. Make sure you know exactly what medical conditions are excluded from your policy if you have had to declare a previous illness.
- **Long-term treatment.** Many insurers place limits on cover for chronic conditions and treatments such as asthma, diabetes, kidney dialysis, bone marrow transplants and heart disease, as well as HIV or AIDS. Psychiatric treatment, including that for eating disorders, may also be subject to exclusions.
- **Maternity and pregnancy.** If it's likely that you might start or expand your family while you're away, check the qualifying period before cover starts. Also investigate whether it includes both routine

pregnancies and ones with complications and treatment of birth defects.

- **Choice of practitioner.** Some policies insist on the use of hospitals and clinics from their own list; you may have to pay if you choose somewhere else.
- **Acts of terrorism.** Innocent bystanders are usually covered, but not always.
- **Dental treatment.** Generally, only emergencies are covered. If you want more, you'll have to pay for it.
- **Acts of God.** Read the small print to make sure injuries arising from natural disasters are covered. They're not always.
- **Guaranteed renewal.** Ensure you will be able to renew your policy without increased premiums if during its term you make a claim or are diagnosed with anything requiring long-term treatment.
- **Excess.** Premiums can be reduced if you agree to pay a certain proportion of a claim. Usually, this is calculated on a per treatment basis, occasionally it's per visit, which obviously might be expensive if a doctor has to see you several times. It can also be assessed from annual claims, but this happens rarely.

INTERNATIONAL JOB HUNTING

The Internet has certainly enabled international job hunting in a way that was simply impossible before. In theory, applying for a post online is the same whether it's based in Newcastle or New Delhi. Either way you won't be waiting, as people used to, for the postman to bring the letter that you'd open with shaking hands.

In the past, you'd look through the limited numbers of overseas jobs advertised in British or international newspapers and specialist professional magazines. Applying directly to companies meant first finding the appropriate person to contact, which isn't so easy when paper directories are usually out of date and perhaps you don't speak the same language as the person on switchboard. Then you had to guess how long the letter of introduction would take to arrive before you followed it up with a phone call.

The modern way of finding work abroad sounds much simpler. Monster (www.monster.co.uk) claims to be the only truly international jobs board representing employers and employees across the world. Alan Townsend, chief operating officer for UK and Ireland, explains: 'Monster's sites in Europe offer jobs in every industry and at every level, from intern to CEO. A global search facility enables job seekers to search for jobs across a wide range of industries, throughout different markets. In addition, Monster has a sophisticated search engine and filtering capability to help employers find the most suitable candidates. You can also carry out pinpointed searches specifying postcode area or region in countries worldwide, enabling both job seekers and employers to find the right jobs and candidates.'

In other words, all you have to do is decide where you want to work and what you want to do, then wait for the job advertisement e-mails to start dropping into your mailbox. There is much to recommend this approach.

No longer do you have to trawl through newspaper pages filled with largely irrelevant job advertisements. Neither do you have to wait until the day that the magazine or newspaper publishes its recruitment supplement.

For certain types of job, it's probably a very effective method. It's best suited to occupations that have clearly defined qualifications, such as medicine or IT. Also if you're looking for a vacancy in the public sector, it's likely that there's a mandatory obligation on organisations to advertise posts.

In the private sector, advertising to fill a post can often be the last resort. Jobs are given to direct contacts or on the recommendation of trusted friends and colleagues. The formal process of recruitment is frequently regarded as expensive, time-consuming and not particularly effective.

Rather than advertising for themselves, organisations will try and find suitable candidates. One place they can look is on sites such as Monster, where you and other suitably qualified people have posted CVs and details. At an executive level, it may also be worth passing your details to a head-hunter. They can be effective. There are also other methods of self-promotion online, which are investigated in the chapter on networking.

The problem, to be honest, with job hunting purely online (either abroad or at home) is that on its own it generally doesn't work. You should only look upon it, at most, as a starting point. It's very easy to spend and waste a great deal of time visiting recruitment and newspaper websites and applying for jobs overseas. You can email hundreds of companies with your details then back it up with a really sophisticated online presence including a great personal website, LinkedIn profile and Facebook page. But don't be surprised if you don't receive a single reply.

It's certainly easier on your nerves to e-mail somebody and ask them for a job than it is to phone them. But it's even easier for them to delete your e-mailed application. Even if you do get a reply, few people are willing to recruit somebody completely sight unseen. You're competing with candidates who live locally and can visit the office for an interview fairly quickly.

Generally, the most effective approach is physically to get to the place where you want to work. That might mean taking a couple of weeks' holiday there or even taking a more menial job in order to be immediately available when the right opening becomes available. There's no shortage of successful

British expats who started by teaching English, to use the most common example.

If you are going on a short trip, make sure you make the most of it. Use every available contact you have. Look up friends, acquaintances, relatives no matter how distant, former work colleagues, people you know from physical or online networking organisations . . . there's no connection too tenuous. Then load your days and nights with as many meetings as you possibly can. Don't worry too much about overbooking, as some people will undoubtedly pull out. And don't think you're wasting their time. Remember, you're the one who has made the effort to fly over to see them.

When arranging to meet contacts who are in your line of business, but probably can't offer you a job, it might be an idea if you can get together in a bar or wherever they socialise after work. You never know where you going to make the contact who will be able to offer you a job and introductions always beat cold-calling as a way to meet people.

Incidentally, if you should find yourself at a loose end one evening, try and get along to one of the bars where expats hang out. The best way of finding out where they are is to ask on one of the online forums before you leave the UK. If not, a few minutes with the local *Yellow Pages* should give you a pretty good idea of which names are likely to be British or Irish. These places are amazingly useful sources of information. Just make sure you can remember the following morning what that useful information was.

During the day, it's also worth making appointments to see the local or British chamber of commerce, if there is one. The same goes for any local organisations related to your occupation. Even if your experience of these bodies in the UK has been somewhat unedifying, in other countries they may be rather more dynamic and serve as the focus of a vibrant local business community. They'll add to your list of contacts anyway.

When you return to the UK, make sure you follow up every lead and business card. E-mail everybody you met and thank them for their time. If anything concrete was discussed, make sure it's now in writing. And, don't forget again that e-mails are easier to ignore than phone calls.

And the follow up process doesn't stop there. Don't let yourself be forgotten. You may feel that you're becoming annoying. Perhaps you are.

But there aren't many times when an employer says: 'I would have given him a job, but he kept pestering me.' The chances are that anybody who complains isn't able or willing to offer anything in the first place.

You may need to be patient, but keep trying. There's frequently a large element of luck in finding the right job in the right place. But it's amazing how often persistence leads to good fortune.

TIPS FOR JOB HUNTING OVERSEAS

- Be organised and methodical. Try to keep track of people you've spoken to, when they said they'd reply and contacts they've recommended. A program such as Microsoft Outlook can be set with reminders and notes about your contacts.
- Make sure your qualifications are valid in the country where you plan to move. You may need to take additional exams before you can work.
- Ensure your degree is recognised. Some countries regard the English three-year degree as being inferior to their own four-year courses.
- Clarify your legal position. It's no good looking for jobs in a foreign country if you're not going to be granted the right visa or work permit, or if it's going to take so long for you to go through the process that it would be too late to take up the offer. It may be that you can start applying for a visa at the same time as you start applying for jobs.
- Check that you understand exactly what is meant in a job advertisement. An 'engineer' in Canada, for instance, means specifically somebody with an engineering degree.
- Tailor your CV. Look online to see examples of how locals present themselves. Is the emphasis on academic qualifications, professional achievements or personality? How long should it be? Which information comes first?
- Do your research. Find out all you can about companies and organisations you might work for and their competitors. Read the local papers online. If you're going to be meeting somebody, put their

name through Google and see what turns up. The more you know about them and their company, the more impressed they'll be.

- Know what you want. Think about what it is you want for your career and then start looking for a match. Bending your requirements simply to live in the sun is unrealistic and the dream often turns sour when boredom or frustration, born from a poor job match, set in.
- Find out what the local rates of pay are. At some point in any job discussion the question of salary will arise. Ask for too much and your prospective employer may back off. Ask for too little and they'll wonder why you're so cheap. Finding figures isn't always that easy, but sometimes local professional magazines run surveys or there are official statistics. Try putting the question into Google for a start.
- Find any gaps in your skills. Looking through job advertisements may reveal a hole in your CV that can easily be filled by a short course.

WORKING REMOTELY

We call ourselves 'digital nomads', 'global telecommuters', 'international virtual workers' or some other vaguely glamorous sounding name. Actually we're just people who work from home, except that home is no longer in the UK.

I can clearly remember when the penny dropped for me. I was sitting in front of my computer in my dressing gown, unshaven. It was 4pm and already almost dark. I hadn't set foot outside for three days. I had no need to venture onto Edinburgh's cold, wet November streets. My work, and most of my life, was reduced to a screen, 19 inches corner to corner, and a telephone.

Then something clicked. I really didn't need to be here. If most of the human contact necessary to earn a living could be made via phone and Internet, I could be anywhere. So I started to formulate a plan. There was nothing to stop my wife Barbara and I taking off to Ibiza for a year, celebrating my 50th birthday along the way. We had a small inheritance after my father died which, as long as I continued to earn something, would tide us over. We could put most of our belongings into my 'home-office' and let our flat out as a two-bedroom which would, hopefully, cover most of the rent for a place in the sun.

In fact, nothing worked out exactly as planned. Thanks to a couple of periods when our Edinburgh flat was empty, we didn't make quite enough to cover the rent on our Ibiza apartment. More importantly we learned how difficult it is to go back.

Physically it would have been fairly easy. It was just a matter of shipping back a few boxes of stuff. But I'd actually got to the point where, as much by accident as by design, I'd ended up as a global telecommuter, earning my income in the UK but living by the Mediterranean. I was editing a major website, writing regularly for a number of publications and acting as a confidential consultant on website content for several large private and public-sector organisations.

Part of my strategy was to make it look as if I was in Britain while I was really in Ibiza. It was simple. I'd leave a phone line in Edinburgh on permanent divert to my home in the sun. After all, few people actually saw me in the course of work. I was just a disembodied voice on the phone, or words in an e-mail.

Despite my already virtual work existence, I was concerned that moving a few thousand miles away would be a psychological barrier for the people who pay for my services. Setting up a diversion wouldn't be expensive, just line rental and, at most, 4p a minute for calls transferred to Spain. Using a cheap 'carrier pre select' (CPS) service meant I wouldn't even have to pay BT's international rates.

Of course, nothing's simple. For a start, BT's diversions have to be set up from the home phone, but I didn't know what my Spanish number was going to be. And, by the time I had a line set up, my Edinburgh flat was being let out in order to pay the rent in Ibiza.

Then, once the diversion was apparently working properly, I couldn't understand why the phone would ring once and stop. It turned out business contacts were fooled by the Spanish ring tone's similarity to the British engaged tone. When I did manage to grab the phone before the caller hung up, there would be complaints about a disconcerting echo on the line. I quickly gave up pretending to be in the UK, but, much to my surprise, being by the Mediterranean often worked in my favour. I was living the dream of many of my business contacts and they seemed to enjoy having somebody to moan to about the weather. Suddenly I also went from being a techie hack to being somebody vaguely exotic.

But actually, even within the space of a few months, the technology has advanced to the point where nobody needs to know where in the world I am when they phone me. That's the wonder of Internet telephony.

I've been a Skype enthusiast almost since it launched in 2004. Computer-to-computer calls over broadband are generally of a much higher quality than ordinary phone calls. They're also free. That makes Skype great for keeping in touch. But, even though you can now make and receive Skype calls to or from a landline, you still have to keep a computer switched on. And a headset remains the best way to use Skype.

Now, I don't mind that call centre look. But really what I want is a substitute phone service and Vonage is the best I've found so far. It comes with a box which hooks up to your broadband router, then you plug in an ordinary phone. That's it. Because I bought it in Britain, it behaves as if that's where I am. I have an Edinburgh number and a subscription which allows me to make unlimited calls to UK landlines for less than £7 a month.

To all intents and purposes, I have now created a situation where I live in Ibiza and work in Scotland. Recently I interviewed two venture capitalists, one apparently in Edinburgh, the other in Aberdeen. In fact they were both in London. It was only after the inevitable ice-breaking conversation about the weather that we all admitted that phone diversions meant we weren't where we seemed to be. The difference was they were in city offices with the prospect of either an impersonal hotel room or hours of trains, planes and automobiles. I was already where I wanted to be.

I'm certainly not alone. There's no shortage of people who have discovered that they can continue their careers where the sun always shines. Generally self-employed knowledge workers, they can ply their trade anywhere with access to e-mail, cheap phone services and budget airlines. And that includes much of Europe.

Stephen and Jaki White moved to Ibiza from Manchester in the late 1980s with sufficient savings from his job as an accountant and hers as a business advisor to earn nothing for their first six months on the island. Stephen completed a course in teaching English as a foreign language which now provides him with a part-time income.

'What I didn't expect,' he says, 'is that there would be a continuing demand for my skills from the UK. I get stuff sent over by e-mail and do some number crunching on it and send it back by e-mail. It's easy.'

What makes Stephen unusual amongst the ranks of globetrotting consultants is that he has not set foot off Ibiza for four years, although he is planning a short break in Valencia. More normally, people choose to base themselves close enough to an international airport to allow for face-to-face meetings.

Xavier Adam, with a UK degree in public relations and a Spanish degree in journalism, runs his agency from bases in the north and south of England,

and in Spain. Asked which one he regards as home he pauses: 'I'm not sure. I catch planes like buses and make sure everything I need for work is stored on the Web so I can access it from anywhere I happen to be.'

And the appearance of foreign telecommuters is not always unpopular with locals. Structural engineer Andy Beeton won an innovation award from the Livradois National Park in central France for helping to stimulate business in the area. He provides technical design services, mainly for UK engineering projects.

'Originally we dealt directly with clients and now we sub-contract and we don't have to deal directly with the public. We do calculations for more or less any building except bridges: commercial, domestic and light industrial. I e-mail the drawings and the calculations to customers, who are often one-man bands and hard pressed to employ someone full time,' he says.

YOUR DESK IN THE SUN

If you're a knowledge worker, there's a good chance you can earn a living without being tethered physically to the UK. There are writers, graphic designers, accountants, day traders, Web designers, marketers, software engineers and people doing a huge variety of jobs where most of their clients and customers are in the UK, but they're in another country.

If you're planning to join them, there are a few things you should think about as you make the move:

1. **Make sure you've got broadband Internet access.** This is now the single most important service you require. Running water's nice, electricity can come from a generator, but dial-up is no substitute for broadband. Don't be fobbed off with promises of future connections, either: sign a lease only once you've seen the broadband connection in action.

2. **Check your transport connections.** If you're relying on being able to nip back to Britain on a fairly regular basis, make sure there are flights. Budget flights to tourist destinations may not be as frequent outside the holiday season.

3. **Set up a separate room as a home office.** Don't double up a bedroom and study. You can't work if there are friends and relatives sleeping in your office. If they want to visit, you can point them in the direction of the hotel down the road.

4. **Don't try and work full-time from a laptop.** For a start you'll feel as if you're only temporarily working in your new offices, then you'll get RSI and finally you'll wreck your machine when you spill coffee on the keyboard. Get a desktop computer and save the laptop for when you're actually travelling.

5. **Get yourself a UK landline number.** If you buy an Internet phone such as Vonage (www.vonage.co.uk) or one from Tesco, it'll come with a choice of British numbers. Plug the box into the broadband router in your new home and the phone will work in exactly the same way as it did in the UK. And you'll get cheap calls too.

6. **Set up a UK mobile phone divert.** A service such as Yac (www.yac.com) will send faxes and phone calls to just about any number you choose. For people contacting you it costs slightly more than calling a UK mobile phone. You pay nothing. And nobody need know that you're not in Britain.

7. **Buy an accounts package for your computer and start tracking income and expenditure as soon as you start planning your business.** Sooner rather than later, you're going to have to register your business and begin paying taxes. You'll need something to show your accountant.

8. **Set up a personal website. It's very cheap and doesn't need to be complicated.** It can even just be a single page outlining what you can offer in terms of work. It will also provide you with your own personal email address which looks far more professional than 'eddiek123@yahoo.com'.

9. **Keep in touch. Find an excuse to phone or email your contacts in the UK on a regular basis.** Most of them will envy you, although they may think you're bonkers. The main thing is you shouldn't be forgotten when there's a chance of some work.

10. **Go out.** Believe me, it's dead easy to shift your computer without moving your life. A computer screen looks the same in Spain as it does in Britain.

CASE STUDY

It's easy to get the feeling that every emigrant from Britain is heading for nature's wide open spaces. Has there ever been one of those interminable fly-on-the-wall television documentaries that has featured a family, couple or singleton moving to a big, dirty city? In every programme I've seen – and I've seen too many – the escapees have headed for a foreign holiday coast or some rural idyll filled with crumbling property, picturesque peasants and unspoilt scenery. (You can switch those adjectives around into any order to get the picture. Peter Mayle has a lot to answer for.)

But there are urbanites who prefer to swap one city for another, and not just because they've been posted there by their company. Felicity Vaughan, for instance, left Edinburgh for Italy about a year ago, but instead of following the usual middle-class dream route to Tuscany's rolling hills, she took her now eight-year-old daughter Rebecca to Rome.

'I wouldn't want anybody to think I was trying to escape from anything. I did want Rebecca to experience the joy of travelling, but it wasn't because I felt any need to get away from Edinburgh. I still love the city and I've had some great times there,' she told me.

It was while in Scotland's capital city that she and two partners set up EcoYoga, (www.ecoyoga.co.uk) a company I at first thought was an Ab Fab spoof. I mean, how much more hippy-capitalist can you get than making and selling the world's only fully biodegradable yoga mats? The others, apparently, are made mainly from PVC which lies around in landfill sites for millennia after it's been full-lotused to death by would-be Madonnas.

At first, EcoYoga sold mainly direct, meaning Felicity spent much of her time packing the jute and latex 'ecomats', then humping them down to the local post office. Then the partners took the decision to drop the retail side and focus entirely on wholesale. They now have a network of distributors around the globe.

Although it wasn't the reason for the change, the effect was to turn the partnership into a virtual business. The postal address might be Edinburgh, but the manufacturing's carried out in Wales, Felicity's in Italy, one partner's on the rural west coast of Scotland and the other's in India for much of the time.

'I spend my working time in Rome in very much the same way as I did in Edinburgh,' says Felicity. 'I'm on the phone or using email to place orders, chase new business and make sure our existing customers are happy. It's very much a case of "have laptop, will travel".'

As with many of the new breed of virtual commuters, her choice of new home was not exactly a carefully-considered decision. 'I went to Rome for five days and just felt "this is a place I want to live". I was obviously a bit concerned about Rebecca, but on the flight back I happened to sit next to a primary school teacher and I told her what I was thinking of doing. She said: "just do it". We parted company at Prestwick baggage handling and I never saw her again. It would be nice to tell her we have done it."

On her return Felicity immediately set to work searching online for an apartment to rent and an international school for Rebecca. 'We got the last remaining place in the school I found. I took that as another sign that this was what we should be doing,' says Felicity.

So, what we have is a single mother taking her young child on a whim to a country where she knows nobody and she doesn't speak the language. If this was television there'd be a nice crisis at this point. Near disaster always strikes in escape-to-the-sun documentaries, generally just before a commercial break or the closing credits. Other people's discomfort is so much more fun to watch than their pleasure. But there are no good television moments from Felicity and Rebecca, who have comfortably survived a year of the Eternal City. I get the feeling, however, that this might not be the final stop on their travels. The technology that allows telecommuters to work from anywhere with a dial tone also removes the need for a final destination.

KEEPING IN TOUCH WITH NETWORKS

When you move abroad it's very easy to be 'out of sight, out of mind', but you needn't be. Far from being forgotten, it's easy to keep in touch with old friends, clients and contacts. You can even broaden your UK circle. And they might continue to offer you work.

The secret is creating, maintaining and developing online networks. It's an awful lot quicker, cheaper and easier to keep in touch than it used to be when all that was available were postcards, letters and expensive phone calls. The main problem is simply keeping up with developments, as 'social networking' is one of the fastest growing areas of Internet technology. Sometimes it's called 'Web 2.0'.

Actually, social networking isn't that new, even on the Internet. Ever since the first e-mails were sent, people have found online ways of putting their points of view across. Whether these are called 'discussion forums', 'bulletin boards', 'mailing lists' or 'social networks', they all serve the same purpose: exchanging information, whether serious or trivial.

For anybody thinking of moving abroad, these networks are absolutely invaluable. As soon as you start to consider a particular area as your new home, look for the local websites and discussion forums. Some are listed at the back of this book, but there are thousands to choose from. There are ones that are focused on a fairly small area and others that are part of a much larger site, perhaps aimed at British expats.

Finding them is a matter of trawling through Google or another search engine. Type in all the variations of the names of the towns, region and country that you are interested in and most sites should show up. The good thing is that the sites that are hardest to find are also likely to be the least active.

Once you've joined, don't be afraid to ask questions, but do check they haven't been answered already. If, for instance, there's a specific document required by foreigners in that region, it's a bit annoying for the people who run the forum to be asked by endless visitors how to get hold of it. Search the site before you post.

Matters of opinion are different. Asking what the schools in the area are like, for example, will probably elicit plenty of responses and may start a debate. Part of the point is to become part of the online community. A word of caution, though: as with any other group of people, some are more vociferous than others. Without seeing them face-to-face it's sometimes hard to work out who has the most valuable opinions.

It is, however, extremely useful to have at least a small group of acquaintances in the place where you're moving to. You may not like them, but with any luck they'll introduce you to people you do get on with. The more people you know, the more likely you are to find like-minded friends.

While you are developing networks at your destination, don't neglect your friends, contacts and business colleagues in the UK. Not only can they help to ease the loneliness which you may experience when you move, but they may be able to provide work both in your new country and if you decide to return to Britain later.

Of course, not everybody's a member of an online network, but not many people, especially of working age, are without an e-mail address these days. So, in the months before you leave, start collecting addresses from anybody who might be interested in knowing what you're up to. A formal newsletter may seem a little egocentric and impersonal, but judicious use of cut and paste can help you to create a large number of personal e-mails fairly quickly.

It's also worth considering creating a blog tracking your move. The technology really is simple. Honestly. If you can use a word processor then you can use, for instance, Blogger software (www.blogger.com) or one of the many other programs you'll find online. A blog is essentially just a diary, but because it's on the Web you can include pictures, links to other useful sites and allow people to respond to your postings. People even make money from blogging by including advertising such as Google's AdSense. It's unlikely to make you rich, but it's very easy to set up.

The easiest way of letting the world know about your blog is simply by including a link in your e-mail signature so that anybody who is interested can see what you are up to. A little caution, however, is needed here. If your move abroad has enabled you to fulfil a lifetime's ambition to become a pole-dancing transvestite drug dealer, it's perhaps not best to advertise this to your former colleagues in the accountancy profession, especially if you're hoping to get some freelance work out of them.

On a professional level, it is worth keeping an eye on both official and unofficial websites linked to your line of business. Some of these sites have quite active forums or e-mail newsletters. Use them. The same goes for any directories where you can put your name and contact details.

You may wonder why there has been a focus on these smaller groups when the big news has been the massive networking sites, often with millions of members, such as MySpace, Ecademy, LinkedIn, Facebook, Friends Reunited, Xing and many others. These virtual communities certainly shouldn't be ignored.

To a large extent, their closest relation in the physical world is a bar. In the same way an establishment will tend to attract drinkers from a particular age group or with a certain interest, the networks appeal to people who have a particular identity and hope to gain something specific from their membership. MySpace, for example, has a strong bias towards pop music and entertainment, whereas LinkedIn is very much more geared to business and IT in particular. So there's not much point in setting up a MySpace page if you're a 45-year-old software engineer hoping to find work contacts unless you've got a band on the go as well.

There's another similarity between virtual communities and trendy boozers. Both go in and out of fashion with dizzying speed. But in the same way that the fact nobody you know goes to your favourite bar doesn't stop you going for a drink after work, neither should a promiscuous attitude to networking sites. Just go with the flow and find out where the people you know or want to meet are hanging out. Many people belong to several communities, perhaps reflecting different facets of their lives.

Now for another word of caution: it's very easy to get caught up in the euphoria of the latest social networking site and to get the feeling that everybody's having a better time than you or, perhaps more importantly in this context, getting more work. Actually, from my experience, very few meaningful or useful relationships are formed which exist only online.

Virtual communities are a good way of staying in touch with friends and business contacts you already know. You may get offers of work from their contacts, but very few people are offered work purely on the basis of their appearance online. Those people must exist somewhere, but I've yet to meet any and I'm fairly active in some of these communities.

The point, then, is to develop your networks face-to-face before you move abroad. If there's a gathering involving potential clients and contacts, you should be there to press the flesh. It isn't easy, especially if (like most people) you're a bit shy. However, it's amazing how far a short chat, a handshake and a business card can go.

There's also a sort of hierarchy of introductions. It's easy to disregard an e-mail, harder to ignore a phone call, more difficult to disregard a physical approach and almost impossible to avoid an introduction from a friend. Of course all that can be replicated in a limited way online, but it's not the same as a physical meeting.

With all this focus on social networking as a business tool, it's easy to forget it can be fun. There isn't a neat dividing line between chatting with friends and making business contacts. They may be the same people. Either way, you'll get most out of your time if you contribute as well as take. If you look at networking as simply a way of marketing your talents, you'll be ignored.

SOCIAL NETWORKS AND VIRTUAL COMMUNITIES

The most useful online networks are probably those linked directly to your occupation or the place where you're planning to live. It is, however, worth looking at the larger online communities as a way of staying in touch. Many are also subdivided into special interest areas.

- **LinkedIn** (www.linkedin.com) is probably the most business-oriented of the large networks. If it has a weakness, it's probably that people tend to become active on it when they're looking for a job, so competition can be intense. Nonetheless it can be a very useful tool.

- **Ryze** (www.ryze.com) offers a slightly different take on business networking. It's worth a look to see if your area of expertise is represented.
- **Ecademy** (www.ecademy.com) is a rather smaller business network, but that might be seen as a strength.
- **Facebook** (www.facebook.com) started off as a way for Harvard University students to stay in touch, but has since been opened up to everybody. As of 2008, it seemed to be on its way to becoming the biggest network in the world, at least for college-educated people.
- **Hi5** (www.hi5.com) may be one you've never heard of, but it's massively popular in South America and parts of Asia.
- **MySpace** (www.myspace.com) is the largest social networking site in the world. Its focus on youth and pop makes it of dubious value for work unless, of course, you're in the music business.

There are hundreds of other networking sites with membership varying from a few hundred into the millions.

EDUCATION

There are some decisions you can never get right. If you decide to stay in Britain for the sake of your children's education, you may have denied them a whole series of life-changing experiences. On the other hand, if you move out of the country there's the possibility that those life-changing experiences will scar them for life. Unfortunately, only time will tell.

If you choose to take your family abroad, you'll be faced with a number of educational options, partly dictated by where you move to, but also by what you can afford. The basic choices are: a local school; an international school; boarding school or home schooling. There's no right choice.

LOCAL AND INTERNATIONAL SCHOOLS

Certainly for people who move overseas under their own steam, rather than being posted abroad by an organisation, sending their children to the local school tends to be the most attractive option. For a start it's a great way to help the family become integrated into the local community.

The children can naturally become bilingual, which is something Brits in particular always envy in other people, because we're so bad at it ourselves. At the same time, there's an assumption that any other country must have a better education system than Britain. This may be partly because we suffered through it ourselves, but also because of the way UK schools and teachers have been pilloried by the media for many years.

But try not to look at the education system in your destination country through rose-tinted spectacles and, if at all possible, find other expats with children who have made the same transition. Don't forget, as well, that you can seldom arrive in a new town and expect to enrol your kids immediately. There's frequently a shortage of places, so try to get your children on the list as soon as you know where and when you're going to be moving.

In a city you may be able to send your children to an international school where the teaching is mainly in English. This may follow the national curriculum for England and Wales or an international curriculum. (See the panel on international educational qualifications at the end of this chapter.) There are, of course, international schools catering to other nationalities and it's possible that in some countries the only places that teach in English follow the US curriculum.

In some ways it's easier for the children of expats to go to an international school. They're surrounded by pupils who have similar backgrounds, share the same language and it's easier to reintegrate into the British education system if the family returns. It's also not unusual for children to ask to be enrolled into an international school after having spent some time at a local primary or secondary.

The most common problem for foreign children in local schools appears to be bullying or, at least, the feeling of being bullied. It's not surprising. Kids are adaptable, but they're also cruel and often fairly intolerant of anybody different. Children face this problem when moving school anywhere, but it feels far worse when you don't speak the language and your best friends are in a different country. Many, if not most, children will have some pain in the transition and a few months can seem like a lifetime when you're young. They'll probably come out the other side with the same feelings about friends and school as anybody else. Some, however, will never settle into a local school.

For parents, deciding when to call it quits and take their child or children out of the local school is extremely difficult. It depends partly on how strong your commitment is to making a life in a new country. There are certainly people who regret having been sent to an international school by their parents. Often they've spent their childhood in a country then decided to stay on, because they feel it's their home. They may have no recollection of Britain at all. Yet their knowledge of the language and culture of the place they live may have been severely restricted by their education. They're foreigners wherever they go.

On the other hand, English is still the most international language in the world. There's a good chance that part of the reason you're able to make a life abroad is because you're a native speaker. Who wants to deprive their children of that same freedom of movement? They may be bilingual, but unless you make a conscious effort to teach them, their spoken English will be fluent as yours, but their writing and grammar may not be up to scratch. A good international school education should enable an academically able child to carry on to university.

First you have to find that good international school. It's not that easy. Assimilating the high turnover of children from expat backgrounds is going to be difficult. In any class there are going to be people who are just starting and others who are about to leave. Also, don't make the assumption that the children will be native English speakers. In China, for instance, having your children educated in English is highly regarded and a status symbol for the newly wealthy. In many international schools there, 80 per cent of the pupils are local Chinese. Elsewhere other non-English speaking expats may prefer to send their children to the international school rather than a local school.

HOME SCHOOLING

If you're moving to somewhere that doesn't have access to an international school, but you're looking to follow a British curriculum, home schooling is another alternative. It could certainly be useful if you're planning for your child to slot back into a UK education system on return.

There are a number of commercial organisations that supply teaching materials for home schooling, as a quick Google search will show you. These are usually organised into packs with lesson plans following the National Curriculum for England and Wales. You can also get support from a personal tutor who should be able to offer support and also an unbiased view of your child's progress.

The materials and lessons don't have to be a complete substitute for local schooling: they can also be used to supplement the standard education your child is receiving while you're abroad. That can mean, however, that the child is spending an awful lot of time working on formal education.

Courses are not hugely expensive, perhaps a few hundred pounds a term. However, the cost in parent's time is high. It's also hard work - even though there are obvious rewards in seeing your child's development and great feelings of achievement when you make an educational breakthrough together.

Equally, though, familiarity can breed contempt. Discipline can be a problem. A teacher has an emotional distance that you can't have. It's not just you. If you've ever seen a teacher who you know rules a class with a rod of iron (hopefully not literally) then watched them with their own uncontrollable offspring, you'll realise the problem is universal.

Home schooling, though, doesn't have to be just one parent and one child. If there are other expat parents in your area, you may be able to spread the load a little by putting two or more kids together. There are also a surprising number of former teachers from Britain who've escaped abroad, but might still welcome a little contact with children, especially if it doesn't involve 25 of the little darlings in a formal classroom setting.

Home schooling can certainly work, but, if you're determined that your child should have a 'proper' English education (or Scottish, Welsh or Northern Irish for that matter), a further alternative is to send them to boarding school in Britain. Some children thrive on the experience.

BOARDING SCHOOLS

If you do decide to pursue this form of education it's important to start looking early, at least a year in advance if possible. This is not only because many schools fill up, but also possibly to take advantage of any financial support that may be available. Boarding schools tend to be very expensive, but there may be bursaries to enable parents to pay the fees of children who would not otherwise be able to attend the school, or scholarships for the most academically able. You may even be able to combine the two.

It's obviously best if you can visit the school with your child. Indeed some insist that pupils are interviewed and tested in person. A few will accept children on a recommendation from an overseas school.

Although you can choose from any boarding school in the country, however, most insist that pupils have an appointed guardian who will provide a home for the child to visit on weekends off, at half term or if there's no convenient flight to the parents' home at the end of term. Guardians are usually relatives or close friends of the pupil's family and it's obviously necessary for them to live within a reasonable distance of the school.

INTERNATIONAL EDUCATIONAL QUALIFICATIONS

Many international schools and some British independent schools offer courses leading to qualifications which are acceptable for admission to university in many countries. These are the main certificates which are usually completed at the age of 18:

International Baccalaureate

The most widely recognised certificate is the International Baccalaureate, offered in over 120 countries. The two-year course allows students to complete their country's qualifications as well as those for the International Baccalaureate. The curriculum is designed to combine the best of many national educational systems.

Students take a course in five areas:

1. **Home language:** covering oral, written and reading skills, along with literature.
2. **Second language:** written and spoken.
3. **Individuals and societies:** includes geography; history; economics; business and management; information technology; philosophy; psychology or social and cultural anthropology.
4. **Experimental sciences:** biology, chemistry, physics, environmental systems or design technology.
5. Mathematics and computer science.

Students have to complete three of these courses at advanced level. They also have to study other cultural perspectives; take part in sports, arts or community service and write an extended essay based on their own research.

The International Baccalaureate is very highly rated academically and recognised by universities everywhere for the purposes of admission. It is a very rigorous course. Visit www.ibo.org for more information.

European Baccalaureate

The European Baccalaureate was designed with the needs of the children of staff of the European Union in mind. They receive free education at

European Schools in Luxembourg, Belgium, Germany, Italy, the Netherlands, Spain and Britain.

The seven-year European Baccalaureate includes study of a main and 'first foreign' language, history, geography, maths, science, ethics/religion and physical education. Some history and geography is taught in the first foreign language. The European Baccalaureate is equivalent to a secondary-school certificate from any EU country.

French Baccalauréat

There are French *lycées* in a number of countries where the Baccalauréat is taught. There are several types of Baccalauréat depending on the academic subjects:

- **L:** French, languages or arts, philosophy, history and geography
- **ES:** Economics and social sciences, mathematics, history/geography
- **S:** Mathematics, physics/chemistry, earth and life sciences

An International Option Baccalaureate is open to multilingual students, which includes courses based around a second language and culture. British students, for instance, can study British literature and history instead of French.

The 'Bac' is a tough three-year course completed with a national exam. It gives automatic entrance to a French university and is widely respected throughout the world for university admission.

British GCSE/A-Levels

There are schools throughout the world offering the British curriculum. Students study widely until they reach 14 when they choose eight to 12 subjects. At the age of 16 they take exams at GCSE (General Certificate of Secondary Education) level.

They then study for four or five AS-levels for a year, then up to four of these as A2-levels. Most UK university courses require three A-level passes. A-levels are also widely accepted and respected by academic institutions across the world.

US High School Diploma

Where there is a large American population, International Schools may offer the US High School Diploma. The problem is that the US has no national curriculum. So there's an emphasis by American schools on problem-solving skills, mastery of core academic subjects and a well-rounded approach to learning.

Gifted students can join Advanced Placement courses which are taught at university level. There are national exams covering 19 Advanced Placement subjects which are highly regarded internationally. They are not required, however, by US universities, which admit students on a combination of high school course grades, letters of recommendation, extracurricular activities and a written essay.

More useful websites

European schools:
www.eursc.eu

US International schools:
www.iss.edu

International Schools Directory:
www.schools.ac

International Schools Association:
www.isaschools.org

MOVING WITH CHILDREN

A change of country is incredibly stressful for kids. Depending on their age, they have less understanding of time, distance and permanence than adults. There are, however, ways in which you can ease the transition for children.

TEN TIPS FOR BEFORE YOU GO

1. Encourage your children to become interested in the place they're going to be moving to. Look for websites, books, brochures, DVDs and television programmes which will help them to get excited about the new country. (You may, however, have to do a little censorship if there's anything scary amongst the material.)

2. Discover the attractions for children at your destination such as zoos, funfairs and shops. Visit their websites with your family.

3. Many DVDs have a choice of languages, so try watching their favourite cartoon or other programme in the language of the country you're moving to.

4. Join with them to take as many pictures as you can of your current home and its surroundings. It's fun and it'll help to provide some comforting images in their new home.

5. Give them an address book and encourage them to collect as many of their friends' contact details as possible. These could include

e-mail addresses, MySpace pages, instant messenger names and even 'snail mail' addresses. (But beware of phone numbers, landline or mobile, for obvious reasons.)

6. Get them to make a collection of pictures of their friends with their pets or brothers and sisters.

7. Work with them to create a list of all the people they want to say goodbye to such as relatives, other children and teachers. Then make sure they follow it through.

8. Encourage them to start planning how their new room will be decorated after the move.

9. Have them divide up their belongings into what they want to take, what should be thrown away and what can be given away. Don't stop them bringing at least some toys which are past their best. There's a reason they look like that.

10. Talk to them about their hopes, fears and expectations about the move. Encourage them to ask you questions.

FIVE TIPS FOR WHEN YOU ARRIVE

1 Especially if you've got small children, the first thing you should do is check your new home for potential danger spots.

2 Visit the attractions you discovered on the Web – and encouraged your children to get excited about – as soon as you reasonably can.

3 You'll be incredibly busy, but do take time to listen and share your children's experiences, especially when they start at their new school.

4 If you've got an Internet connection, encourage them to keep in contact with their old friends, but discourage them from spending too long online with them. A little contact can be comforting, but too long can make the transition slower and more painful.

5 Don't force them to go out alone, even if you've moved to a very safe area, until they feel secure. A big move like this can give even a cocky teenager a crisis of self-confidence.

WHAT TO DO WITH YOUR UK PROPERTY

Moving abroad can turn expats into accidental landlords and property speculators. If you own your home, what do you do with it if you leave the country?

Some people will find that they can sell their home in the UK, pay off the mortgage and have enough left to buy a property abroad, or at least put down a substantial deposit. It may seem to be the perfect solution, but it does mean relinquishing a spot on the British housing ladder. That doesn't matter so much if property prices in the new country of residence rise faster than in the UK, but nobody can predict the market with certainty.

Alternatively, you can let your British home and use the income to rent a foreign property. For anybody planning a move overseas of just a few years, this is often the best approach. It is, however, not without its potential pitfalls. For a start, income cannot usually be guaranteed for more than six months and if there are gaps between tenancies, no money will be coming in. Expenditure, meanwhile, will probably rise as council tax may have to be paid and there's the cost of advertising for new tenants along with, perhaps, decorating and replacing worn-out fittings.

Even with these dips in income to contend with, many expats have done rather nicely out of their UK properties, thanks to the steep rise in prices over the last few years. Effectively they've become part of the buy-to-let business. It's often those with the largest mortgages that have done best. But do beware of Capital Gains Tax, which is discussed later.

The economics of buy-to-let are easy to understand, but that doesn't mean they're without risk if the housing market slips. Imagine a property initially worth £100,000. After a year, its value rises to £105,000. If you own it outright, your investment has brought a five per cent return. But with a 50 per cent mortgage, your initial investment is £50,000 so a £5,000 rise now represents a ten per cent gain, assuming rent covers the monthly payments to a bank or building society. Then if you had an 80 per cent mortgage and the rest of the figures remained the same, your annual profit would be 25 per cent.

Don't get too excited though at this apparently brilliant investment opportunity. It's unlikely that the UK property market will continue to grow at the rate it has in recent years. If prices fall, the high percentage profits in the last paragraph become high percentage losses. And, anyway, the profit or loss only matters if you sell your UK home. That's an important point to remember.

People who buy a property to let are buying an investment, not a home. They'll choose a location where rents are high relative to prices. It doesn't matter to them whether it's a place they'd want to live. Furniture, fixtures and décor will be chosen to maximise rental income. Investors can still have bad tenants who fall behind with the rent and damage the property, but the cost is financial not emotional.

It can all go horribly wrong for expats. Kay and David McMahon have chronicled their tale of woe online at www.trashedhouse.com. Four years after being posted abroad, they tried to return to their London home, a process that took months of legal wrangling, and when they finally regained possession the place was uninhabitable.

It wasn't that the McMahons hadn't used a reputable firm of letting agents; they had. But there does seem to be something fundamentally flawed about that whole process. The problem is that rental agencies are servants of two masters. There are the landlords, who may be thousands of miles away, and the tenants, who live nearby. With the best will in the world, it's easy to see who is likely to get the best service: the tenants who are handing over their cash every month.

At the same time, there are less obvious costs than seemingly exorbitant fees charged by agencies. Most accidental landlords let out their homes as furnished accommodation. It's simpler legally and saves on the cost of shipping furniture that may be cheaper abroad.

What this doesn't account for is the mass of small items such as linen and kitchen utensils which you have to provide for tenants and then buy again in your new home. It's amazing how expensive it all turns out to be.

Rather than using a letting agent, some people opt to rent their home to friends or relatives. This will save money on agents' fees, but can equally create other problems. An informal agreement can be matched by an informal attitude to paying the rent. There's also an inclination to cut the taxman out of the equation, which is always a risky strategy (not to mention illegal). Apart from the danger of being caught, the tenants' financial position may change through unemployment, illness or pregnancy. Without a legitimate rental agreement, they won't be able to claim housing benefit. And if they simply want to leave for some reason, there is the problem of finding new tenants, which may not be easy from thousands of miles away.

Fortunately, although property letting agents may not be perfect and their fees may seem exorbitant, they are tax-deductible.

TAX AND THE EXPAT LANDLORD

Non-resident landlords are liable for tax on income from property rentals in the UK. The allowable expenses are, however, fairly generous. But you won't get them unless you claim, so it is probably worth using the services of an accountant who can help fill in the self-assessment income tax form that anybody receiving income from property must complete.

Deductible expenses include professional agents' fees, accountancy fees, water rates, insurance, repairs and maintenance. For furnished property, ten per cent of rental income can be claimed for wear and tear. There's no limit to allowances for borrowing, usually through a mortgage, when the money is spent to buy or improve a property. Once expenses have been set against receipts there'll be either a profit or loss.

Even if there is a profit, there may be no tax to pay as there are allowances available to many individuals, but they have to find out whether they are eligible and notify the tax authorities. If a property is jointly owned, the profits are divided between husband and wife, which offers a further way of reducing tax liabilities.

Should you decide to sell your British property, you may face capital gains tax (CGT) especially if you will be returning to the UK within five years. The tax is payable on profits from the sale of property or other assets. There is, however, exemption on the sale of your 'principal residence', as the tax office calls your home. Check out all your queries with Revenue and Customs, to be on the safe side (www.hmrc.gov.uk).

REDUCING THE PAIN OF COMING HOME

There's absolutely nothing to be ashamed of if you decide to return to the UK after spending time abroad. You may have planned it that way, but it can be hard to escape the feeling that your friends and colleagues see you as something of a failure. But, don't forget, most of them at some point in their lives will have thought about working overseas. You've justified their inertia.

Anyway, if fear of embarrassment is the only thing preventing your return, get packing now. There's no sense in being miserable in a foreign country for the sake of your ego. If anybody does think any the worse of you, their feelings will pass very quickly.

Actually, in my experience of living overseas, relatively few people do go back even when all their plans have gone awry, usually for financial reasons. The world seems to be full of Brits who have poured the profits from the sale of their homes into businesses that have gone bust. Again, this is nothing to be ashamed of: statistically, most start-ups anywhere in the world are destined to fail. But the boom in property prices which financed the move also makes getting back onto the UK ladder very difficult.

Even when all the mechanisms are all in place for your return, once you've left the UK, it really is difficult to go back. Okay, there will be people reading this who have a carefully planned career strategy which includes one or more postings abroad. Maybe they're in the finance sector and feel that both their CVs and their salaries would be enhanced by a couple of years in China learning Mandarin and finding out what makes the world's most populous economy tick. Perhaps they will return to London, but how long will it be before the banking systems of India, the USA or Japan become an intriguing challenge? Going back is very hard.

In 2003 when my wife and I left Scotland bound for Spain, we had a clear plan. We'd found a beautiful apartment in Ibiza with a 12-month lease which could be paid for (almost) by renting out our flat in Edinburgh. That was it. We'd spend a year in the sun then return to Scotland. Of course, when it came to the crunch we couldn't go back. We may not expect to spend the rest of our lives in the same house we live in now, but our discussions of the future don't feature Scotland's Tupperware skies.

None of this is to say that living abroad is easy unless, perhaps, you've sufficient funds to live independently, in which case this book's not really aimed at you. Its focus is on working abroad. And, if nothing else, earning a living outside the UK will reveal just how much you've taken for granted in your British working life.

It would be handy at this point if I could provide a neat plan which would prepare would-be expats for the changes their going to face. There are 'life coaches' and other forms of relocation counsellor who offer this service. They may be useful, but I must admit that I was always profoundly sceptical about their value. Now that I do live abroad, perhaps I can see that they may provide a useful function.

Some things life coaches have to say may surprise people who haven't spent time abroad. In the course of writing this book, for instance, I spoke to life coach Claire Laborde. She's English and met her French husband when they both worked in Saudi Arabia. They now live in France.

She told me that it often takes three years for problems to manifest themselves after somebody moves abroad. 'Human beings are very adaptable,' she explained. 'There's a honeymoon period when problems will be hidden, then, after about three years, the old problem behaviours will adapt themselves to their new surroundings.'

I would have said that seems a long time, but having been part of an expat community for a while it seems about right. Perhaps what's confusing is the concept of a 'honeymoon period'. Wherever you move to, the length of time that you're a novelty is relatively short.

If you're the only foreigner in the area, or at least one of the few, there'll probably be a phase when you're in great demand. The locals will get to try out their few words of English and find some amusement in the way you strangle their language. But it won't be long before the fun wears off and the lack of communication becomes boring for all concerned. Learning the language as quickly as possible is obviously vital, but you also need to find something to talk about.

In Spain I've found two extremely useful topics. The first is Telefónica, the country's main phone company. Just wander into a bar muttering 'Telefónica' and immediately people will start to tell their tales of woe. All you need to do is shake your head sadly and say *si* or *no* at what seems the appropriate point, and everybody will assume you're fluent in the language. The other topic is, of course, football. A little knowledge of the local team's star names and a few clichés – which generally seem to translate directly from English – and you're part of the crowd. I'm not going to stray into female territory by suggesting conversation topics for women. It'll just get me into trouble.

Moving to somewhere with a big British community will probably lead to your social life following a slightly different trajectory. Communication won't be quite the same problem, although there may be times when you wish it was. You begin with two things in common, nationality and language. And usually that's enough at first. Early relationships are like the ones you have on holiday when couples or families pal around for a couple of weeks. At the end of the fortnight, your worst nightmare is that they'll take you up on your offer to put them up if they're ever in the area. Being an expat can mean never having to say goodbye. Or perhaps that should read, 'never being able to say goodbye'.

Whether you're amongst foreigners or Brits, you will have to work to keep the initial momentum going, maintaining those friendships you value. You are, anyway, into an extended learning period once the first flush of the honeymoon is over. The pace of meeting new people will slow, but it'll probably still be faster than it was in Britain. You'll be facing new problems and solving them one way or another. And that's a big difference. If you're bored and lonely now, you can blame the move. It's not to do with the way you are. And, anyway, there are always new places to go and see, new experiences to enjoy, or not. You're out of the comfort zone.

The need to escape the tyranny of the rat race or the boredom of the routines that dominate their lives drives many people to move overseas. Three years later they're workaholics too busy to enjoy their sunny surroundings or they're in their new home watching British satellite TV or

DVDs. Another common expat difficulty that Claire Laborde pointed out is the change of status. She was talking about people who move to a country where, perhaps because they're not native speakers of the local language, they are unable to find a job commensurate with the one they held in their home country. I certainly know plenty of people in Ibiza who were engineers, doctors and senior office managers who now work as cleaners, drivers or labourers. Actually, most at least start by enjoying the lack of responsibility that comes with these jobs, but that doesn't always last.

It's not just a lower status that Brits abroad can find hard to cope with. Multinational companies may post staff from their headquarters country to run branch offices overseas. This can obviously cause resentment amongst the locals, but the person who has been parachuted in can also feel that perhaps there is no need for them to be there.

And if it's hard for the people who have been posted abroad to work, it can be far more difficult for their partners and children, even if it sounds as if it should be a dream come true. Some postings, for instance, come with a luxury house and even domestic staff. It's not easy to leave behind the status which comes with a career to go somewhere that you no longer even have responsibility for running your home. Status may no longer be related to ability, but to nationality or even colour.

This is only one of the challenges that partners and children can face. In many ways, their readjustment is harder than it is for the person who has been posted abroad. Even if the work is more difficult, at least the skills are likely to be similar to the ones that got them the job in the first place. There'll also be familiar voices and emails from the UK office. Stuck at home, the partner's going to be coping with all sorts of new problems without support. And the problems of expat kids are discussed elsewhere in this book.

Unsurprisingly, it's generally reckoned that the most common reasons for overseas postings ending prematurely relate to problems that the family has in settling in. The employing organisation should be compassionate and it is certainly wrong to make other peoples' lives a misery for the sake of your career or whatever your motivation for the move. On the other hand, time does resolve many problems. Once children, in particular, start to make new friends, life suddenly seems better and often they'll be the ones who want to stay.

For kids, technology can be both a help and a hindrance. The Internet provides instant and often free access to their old friends. Initially that's great, but as time goes on, it can prevent them from letting go of their old lives. And the events being missed seem so much more exciting given the benefit of distance. On the other hand, if you are returning, then maintaining old friendships will make reintegration very much easier.

From a practical point of view, the biggest problem with returning early may be finding somewhere to stay if you've rented your house out. Depending on the lease, it may be several months before you can get back in. It's not an insurmountable difficulty, but it is a hassle.

More awkward could be getting your children back into their original schools. It goes without saying that you should contact the headteacher as soon as you have a rough idea of a return date. You may even consider timing your return to fit in with the school year and perhaps using some home teaching materials (see p. 175) to help your children slot back into the curriculum.

Actually, kids are likely to be the ones who have least difficulty in slotting back in. If parents have been having problems abroad, it will have affected their children as well. Moving back to familiar surroundings may be a relief.

You may also be excited at the prospect of returning to the UK, especially if your time abroad has been tough. Family and friends will initially be thrilled to see you back, although the novelty of your foreign tales can wear off rather quickly. They won't have put their lives on hold waiting for your return.

Readjustment isn't always easy. Even on a brief return to Scotland I felt almost panic-stricken and overwhelmed by the size and quantity of choice in a supermarket. Returning expats report this sort of reverse culture-shock can take a while to get over.

BEFORE YOU RETURN – CHECKLIST

1. Ensure your UK bank accounts and credit cards are active. You don't want to be without access to cash while you go through the lengthy process of opening an account. For that reason, it's generally a good

idea to maintain an account with a British bank or one of its offshore branches.

2. Speak to your accountant or financial advisor about the optimum time for your return to minimise your tax liabilities.

3. To help your credit rating, it's also worthwhile getting back on the electoral roll as soon as possible.

4. Get in contact with schools to ensure they have a place for your children.

5. If you're driving back, make sure you have adequate insurance for your car and belongings. Minimal 'green card' cover will probably not include the vehicle contents.

6. Make sure you have health cover. If you've been outside the UK for some time, you will probably not be entitled to free NHS cover.

7. Try to find out what your position is with benefits. The cost of return may have left you absolutely broke and you may not be returning to a job, but that doesn't mean you'll receive automatic assistance.

8. Contact the British embassy or consulate in the country where you're living if your family circumstances have changed, for instance, if you've had a child abroad, married a foreign national, been divorced or widowed.

9. If you're bringing back a pet, make sure its passport, vaccinations and identification chip are in order.

10. Revive your business and social networks using the Internet, phone and e-mail before you return. Personal contacts are still the best way to get back to work.

100 USEFUL WEBSITES

This is by no means an exhaustive list, but it's a start. The most useful are probably the online communities where expats who have made the move already share their experiences and allow you to learn from their mistakes. The people who contribute to these discussion forums are often incredibly generous with their time, but don't abuse it and try to give something back when you're in the same position. Everybody's an expert when they've made the move. Success or disaster, it's a learning experience for all.

Where there seem to be fairly limited numbers of forums for specific countries, it may be because the action is on one of the huge websites with communities in many regions. You'll just have to spend a little while researching to find which is the best and adding a few searches of your own. One word of warning: don't take as gospel everything you read – even locals can provide information that is inaccurate or out of date. It's particularly difficult to keep track of changes in local bureaucracy.

The same goes for the commercial sites mentioned here. Companies vary in how much priority they give to keeping their websites up to date. The fact they're listed here is not an endorsement, it's just that I've found them interesting or useful.

Finally, the categories used are slightly arbitrary especially when they are large sites covering a number of areas. Just treat them as a starting point, using their links and your favourite search engine.

Area	Website name	URL	Description
General	Steve Kropla's site	www.kropla.com	Where will your mobile, modem and electrical goods work?
General	A Place In The Sun	www.aplaceinthesunlive.com	Online information linked to the Channel 4 overseas property show
General	The Foreign & Commonwealth Office	www.fco.gov.uk	Huge site with profiles of every country in the world and useful information about working in the EU
General	Crown Relocations	www.crownrelo.com	Hong Kong based company used to relocating people all over the world. Useful information on the site
General	Expat Blog	www.expat-blog.com	Hundreds of blogs listed by country. Their quality is variable, but you may find somebody who is already living your dream
General	Just landed	www.justlanded.com	Guides to living and working in a number of countries
General	Expat Web Directory	www.expatwebdirectory.com	Massive collection of links to expat resources with a US bias
General	International Living	www.internationalliving.com	Large US-oriented website, forum and newsletter service
General	Expat Focus	www.expatfocus.com	Patchily-useful collection of guides and articles written by expats
General	Anglo Info	www.angloinfo.com	Doesn't quite live up to its claim to be: 'Everything you need for life in another country . . .' but it's trying
General	Citizens Information	www.citizensinformation.ie	Although aimed at Irish citizens this site is useful for any EU resident
General	Overseas Digest	overseasdigest.com	US oriented, but valuable information on jobs and life abroad with introductory guides to individual countries
General	Overseas Emigration	www.overseas-emigration.co.uk	Agents for emigration to Australia, New Zealand, Canada & USA
General	Expat interviews	www.expatinterviews.com	Large collection of resources for expats including some active discussions
General	A Desk In The Sun	www.adeskinthesun.com	The website created by the writer of this book focusing on international telecommuting
General	Embassy World	www.embassyworld.com	Directory and database of the world's embassies and consulates
General	Claire Laborde life coach	www.clairelaborde.com	Expat life coach
General	Life coaching	www.coachfederation.org	Worldwide resource for business and personal coaches
General	Expat Women	www.expatwomen.com.	Huge and very professional website run by an Australian and an American

General	Guardian Abroad	www.guardianabroad.co.uk	Practical advice and shared company for your international adventure
General	Guardian Weekly	www.guardianweekly.co.uk	Global view of the week's international events combining comment and analysis from the daily *Guardian* newspaper with features from the *Observer*, the *Washington Post* and *Le Monde*
Finance	Robinson Maddock Consulting	www.rmctax.co.uk	Expat tax experts
Finance	HSBC Offshore	www.offshore.hsbc.com	Offshore branch of high street bank with particularly useful information
Finance	The Fry Group	www.thefrygroup.co.uk	Tax and financial advice for expats
Finance	Investor Morse	www.investormorse.com	Offshore investment specialist
Finance	Mazars	www.mazars.co.uk	International tax advisors
Finance	HMRC Residency	www.hmrc.gov.ukcnr	Starting point for information about UK taxation and National Insurance for expats
Finance	Moneycorp	www.moneycorp.com	Cheaper alternative to banks for transferring currencies
Finance	Currency Solutions	www.currencysolutions.co.uk	UK foreign exchange and money transfer specialist
Finance	World of Offshore Banks	www.worldoffshorebanks.com	Huge searchable directory of offshore banking providers
Finance	Universal Currency Converter	www.xe.com	Check how much the world's currencies are worth
Finance	Expat Investor	www.expatinvestor.com	Wide ranging site covering most aspects of expat money with free digital magazine
Finance	Shelter Offshore	www.shelteroffshore.com	Property-oriented guide to expat money
Finance	Offshore Lending	www.offshorelending.co.uk	Brokers for offshore mortgages
Finance	Trashed House	www.trashedhouse.com	The perils of letting your home in the UK
Relocation	International Moving	www.internationalmoving.biz	Price comparison site for international moving companies
Relocation	Expat Exchange	www.expatexchange.com	American-oriented site with global information on relocation
Relocation	Mobility Services International	www.msimobility.com	Trends and developments in the employee relocation industry
Health	Expacare	www.expacare.com	International health insurance
Health	Good Health Worldwide	www.goodhealthworldwide.com	Health insurance for expats
Health	International Health Insurance	www.ihi.com	International and medical health insurance
Health	International SOS	www.internationalsos.com	Worldwide medical services and insurance cover

Education	Gabitas	www.gabbitas.co.uk	Independent advice for parents, including expats, wanting to send children to non-state schools
Education	Teacher Net	www.teachernet.gov.uk	Useful English National Curriculum resources
Education	National Curriculum Online	ttp:www.nc.uk.net	Everything you always wanted to know about Key Stages in England and Wales
Education	Learn Premium	www.learnthings.co.uk	Resources for school or home teaching
Education	Council of International Schools	www.cois.org	Organisation for accreditation of international schools with 500 members
Australia	Working in Australia	www.workingin-australia.com	Jobs-based website with other useful information
Australia	Migration Expert	https:www.migrationexpert.com	Online migration services
Australia	Australian Government Department of Immigration and Citizenship	www.immi.gov.au	Look through the information on this site before paying for any commercial migration services
Australia	Aussie Move	www.aussiemove.com	Comprehensive site for anybody emigrating to Australia
Canada	Citizenship and Immigration Canada	www.cic.gc.ca	Official government site and best starting point for would-be emigrants to Canada
China	China Expat	www.chinaexpat.com	Detailed information and active discussion forums for expats in China
China	Chinese Embassy London	www.chinese-embassy.org.uk	Includes information and forms required for visas and work permits for China
China	Expats in China	www.expatsinchina.com	Wide-ranging information on life and work in China
France	In' pat	www.inpat-france.com	Newcomers guide to Paris
France	Total France	www.totalfrance.com	Active community of Francophiles
France	Lost in France	www.lost-in-france.com	Guide and discussions about living in France
France	Expatica	www.expatica.com	News and information for expats in France
Germany	How to Germany	www.howtogermany.com	Online information resource for expatriates in Germany linked to magazine of the same name
Hong Kong	Hong Kong Immigration Department	www.immd.gov.hk	Official government site with detailed information and forms for visas and work permits
Hong Kong	Asia Expat	http://hongkong.asiaxpat.com	Jobs and property listings for Hong Kong
Italy	Expats in Italy	www.expatsinitaly.com	Active site and forum

Italy	How to Italy	http://howtoitaly.typepad.com/howtoitaly	An American proves that living in Italy needn't slow you down
Italy	The Informer	www.informer.it	Information source for anybody thinking of moving to Italy
Japan	Entrepreneur Association of Tokyo	www.ea-tokyo.comindex.php	Networking for entrepreneurs of all nationalities in Tokyo
New Zealand	Quotable Value	https://www.qv.co.nz	Property prices in New Zealand
New Zealand	Immigration New Zealand	www.immigration.govt.nz	Well-organised government site covering all aspects of moving to New Zealand
Portugal	Portuguese Government	www.portugal.gov.pt	Portuguese government site with plenty of information in English, some of which may be useful
South Africa	Cape Town Chamber of Commerce	www.capetownchamber.com	Useful starting point for anybody wanting to work or do business in South Africa
South Africa	Alive with possibility	www.southafrica.info	Huge website covering most aspects of living working and doing business in South Africa
Spain	This is Spain	www.thisisspain.info	Links, news and information about moving to Spain
Spain	Euroresidentes	www.euroresidentes.com	Living, working or travel in Spain. Information, guides and help
Spain	Spain Business	www.spainbusiness.com	Spanish government-run website for anybody doing business in or with Spain
UAE	Emirates Village	www.emiratesvillage.com	Recruitment and property classified advertisements for the UAE
USA	Immigrate2us	www.immigrate2us.net	Discussion forum on the trials and tribulations of passing through the US immigration service
USA	Path2usa	www.path2usa.com	Very detailed information on all aspects of emigrating to the USA
Business	International Chamber of Commerce	www.iccwbo.org	The voice of world business
Business	Council of British Chambers of Commerce in Continental Europe	www.cobcoe.org.uk	Useful source of information and contacts in many European countries
Business	uktradeinfo	www.uktradeinfo.com	Trade statistics from HM Revenue and Customs. Find your gap in the global market
Business	Eurostat	epp.eurostat.ec.europa.eu	More than you could ever want to know about the European Union in figures
Business	Kwintessential	www.kwintessential.co.uk	Cross-cultural communication experts' with useful information on business etiquette across the globe

Business	Index of Economic Freedom	www.heritage.org	How free is enterprise in the world's economies?
International	British ExPats	http://groups.yahoo.com/group/British-Ex-Pats	Yahoo-hosted forum for expat Brits
International	allo Expat	www.alloexpat.com	Discussion forums for many countries, some are very active, others have less participants
International	Expatriates.com	www.expatriates.com	Active British-oriented online community
International	Easy Expat	www.easyexpat.com	General information for expats in a variety of countries with moderately active discussion forums
International	Expat Network	www.expatnetwork.com	Large collection of resources for expats including some active discussions
International	British Expat	www.britishexpat.com	Vast number of articles and a good starting point for anybody wanting to find information about living anywhere in the world.
International	Expat Focus	www.expatfocus.com	Jobs, property, advice and active forums
Work	Monster	http://globalgateway.monster.com	Gateway to jobs in a variety of countries
Work	MedHunters	www.medhunters.com	Claims to be 'the world's largest healthcare job board'
Work	Eures	http://ec.europa.eu/eures	Job centre for the EU
Work	Career Bridge International	www.careerbridge.com.au	Australia-based site with huge number of links to headhunters and executive recruitment agencies
Work	Work Wise UK	www.workwiseuk.org	Aimed at a UK audience, but with much useful advice on working from home in any country
Work	Goinglobal	www.goinglobal.com	International career information website
Work	Executive Planet	www.executiveplanet.com	Country by country guide to doing business
Work	Payaway	www.payaway.co.uk	Work your way round the world
Work	Expats Direct	www.expatsdirect.com	Global online recruitment agency

INDEX